Bead Embroidery

Written and illustrated by
Joan Edwards

LACIS
Berkeley, California

The following *figure* numbers have been
intentionally deleted in this edition:
141-143, 153-167, 230

First published 1966
© Joan Edwards 1992

This edition edited by Joan Edwards
and published 1992 by:

LACIS

3163 Adeline Street, Berkeley, California 94703, USA

ISBN 0-916896-44-7

Contents

For Joy with love

Wooden doll with beaded hair, Egypt, c. 2000 B.C.
British Museum

Acknowledgment

The encouragement and goodwill of a great many people have gone into the making of this book and to mention individually all those who, with infinite patience and care have answered my numerous and often troublesome questions, would be far too extensive; amongst them are the keepers and assistant keepers in many museums both national and local, as well as the staff at a number of libraries, notably those at the British Museum, the Victoria and Albert Museum, and the Embroiderers' Guild, and also at the Guildhall Library, the Fawcett Library, and the Library of H.M. Customs and Excise.

In the beginning Mr J. L. Nevinson, formerly of the Department of Textiles, Victoria and Albert Museum, introduced me to certain literary sources with which I was then unfamiliar, for I am a designer, a needlewoman and a teacher, not a scholar, and without this initial guidance and his continued interest and criticism, the historical survey I have been able to attempt would have been less comprehensive and certainly less well documented. In this connection I am grateful to Miss M. Holloway for her help in arranging the bibliography. Valuable references were also given me by Miss Anne Buck, Museum of Costume, Platt Hall, Manchester; Dr Sigrid Müller, Bavarian State Museum, Munich; Miss Sarah Neblett, Cornel University, Ithaca, New York and Mr D. Snelgrove, Paul Mellon Foundation for British Art, London.

Much of the technical information was obtained from Whitefriars Glass Limited; from the late Mr W. J. Farrier of the bead importing house of Ells and Farrier Limited; from Mr J. Lock, Associate Member of the Incorporated Society of London Dress Designers; and from Mrs Bagnall who was once a professional beader. Through the good offices of Dr G. Rossel, a partner in the glassmaking firm of Josef Riedel of Vienna, I was able to visit their factory at Kufstein and see the processes involved in making and colouring embroidery beads; and I am grateful for having been allowed access to the records of Messrs Debenham and Freebody Limited whose workroom was once famous for the beauty of its beading.

Amongst my friends I have special reason to thank Mrs C. Shepelef who translated L. I. Yakunina's book on Russian pearl embroidery for me and thus made it possible for a chapter on this little known aspect of the subject to be included; and to Mrs Alice Vagn Jensen, Mrs Joyce Dunsheath, and Miss Mary Kemp who have translated various foreign periodicals and catalogues. Also Miss Hazel Pinder for allowing me to publish her pattern for a beaded Christmas decoration; Mr R. Speight who reconstructed a bead loom from an old diagram; Mrs

Margaret Beautement; her daughter Christine who made the beaded furniture; my cousin Miss Joy Lee who corrected the proofs; and Miss Thelma Nye of B. T. Batsford who has always been at hand to encourage and advise.

The idea that I should write a book on bead embroidery, however, originated with Miss Iris M. Hills who was formerly in charge of the Needlework Development Scheme at Glasgow, under whom I studied as a 'mature' student at the Hammersmith College of Art and Building. To her, and to the lecturers at my first art school in Auckland, New Zealand, I owe far more than a few brief and necessarily formal sentences can express.

JOAN EDWARDS
London 1966

Special to this edition:

Had it not been for the help and interest of my friend Margaret Carey, consultant ethnographer, the urging of many embroiderers and bead workers, and the enthusiasm of Jules Kliot of LACIS, this amended edition of BEAD EMBROIDERY (1966) would not have been possible, and I am sincerely grateful to them all.

Joan Edwards
Dorking 1992

THIS has been a most enjoyable book to write. Beads, which enter into the lives of each of us at one point or another, have a pleasing facility for attracting and interesting everybody. Substantially the same in structure, they exist, nevertheless, in innumerable different shapes, sizes and colours, and for a hundred different purposes. They can be broken but they never wear out. They are unimportant, even trivial things, but as Dr Joan Evans, herself a needlewoman of distinction, has said: 'Much of the civilization of an age can be recorded in the history of trivial things'; and from this angle archaeologists, anthropologists, and historians have all found them to be an invaluable source of scientific information and an abundantly rewarding field of study.

But bead embroidery, or more properly *beads in association with textiles*, is a neglected and almost wholly unexplored corner of the subject, and more than a quarter of a century has passed since a correspondent signing herself *Aiguille* sent the following letter to the editor of *Notes and Queries*:

'From time to time there occurs a revival of interest in beadwork, this usually taking the form of ladies' evening bags. People then bring out specimens from hoards of their grandmother's things, and some take to copying the old designs many of which are very pleasing. Who is the authority on this little branch of needlework? Has anyone written a book about it?'

That no reply was ever received to these questions would appear at first sight to be nothing more or less than my good fortune, a subject not already overloaded with books being very rare indeed these days; but if the inquirer had taken the trouble to search through the Subject Index of the library of the British Museum she could have found these titles: *Bead Furniture and Ornamental Beadwork*, M. Smith (1889); *How to do Beadwork*, M. White (1904); *The Priscilla Beadwork Book*, B. Robinson (1912); and *Beadcraft*, I. B. Littlejohns (1934). There was also a volume of Weldon's *Practical Needlework* series devoted to beadwork, but to all intents and purposes that completes the list she might have made, and none is any longer available to the general reader. Books on this particular method of embroidery are, therefore, virtually non-existent.

This is a challenging position in which to be placed, but it contains certain built-in dangers and of these I have been acutely aware, especially when I found myself working on some historical material concerning the relationship between beads and bugles which has not, as far as I know, been previously examined in connection with this particular subject.

'Beads,' said Mrs A. H. Christie, 'are a fascinating material to work with; all kinds of pretty things can be done with them, either sewing them on a ground, knitting or crocheting them, or making use of a small bead loom' and bead embroidery was ever one of the main standbys of the editors of Victorian magazines which carried page after page of information on how best to practise what they described as 'this graceful occupation and inexhaustible (*sic*) source of laudable and innocent amusement'. Nothing escaped their passion for beadwork, and as the years went by more and more improbable objects became, under their instructions, covered with beads. Repetition was inevitable and the prospect of sifting through the countless bound volumes of their publications that stand in long dusty runs on library shelves is utterly bizarre. I have therefore confined myself almost exclu-sively to scanning *The Englishwoman's Domestic Magazine*, first published by S. O. Beeton and later taken over by Ward Lock and Tyler Limited; and to Godey's *Lady's Book* which commenced publication in Philadelphia in the late 1820s and by 1850 claimed to be the oldest magazine in America.

Just now beads and sequins are available in more various and lovely colours, shapes, and sizes than ever before. They are in fashion again after one of their long periods of enforced retire-ment and neglect, and so the demand for information on how best to use them is con-siderable. This book has been written in an effort to fill this need, but by providing historical as well as practical information, I hope that it will also go some way towards bridging the gap in our knowledge of this very ancient method of embroidery that has for too long yawned, un-occupied, before us.

The use of beads in Egypt goes back to the Neolithic Period, that is, between seven and ten thousand years, and glass beads were made there as early as the fifth century B.C. Elaborate beaded necklaces and belts were one of the features of Egyptian dress and it was by no means unusual for the mum-mified bodies of the dead to be buried wearing a number of necklaces, bracelets and anklets; the mummies were often covered also with beaded nets that were formed by threading long bugle-like beads—generally blue—into a mesh. The illustration shows what are described as 'Cretan tribute bearers each carrying a string of blue and red beads'. They were found at Thebes and are dated between 1475 and 1448 B.C. The drawing was made from Plate V, 'Theban Tomb Series', 5th Memoir, published by the Egypt Exploration Society 1933

General information

Needles and Threads Beading needles are long and pliable. The usual sizes range from 10 to 13. At one time they were known as *straws* and were often made by doubling over and twisting the end of a short piece of very fine wire so that it formed an eye.

The thread used depends on (*a*) the type of embroidery or beadwork, and (*b*) the size of the beads. For embroidery on dress, No. 60 mercerised cotton is generally used in the dress trade.

The thread must be waxed.

Frames As it is difficult to do beading successfully in the hand, the fabric should be stretched over a round or tambour frame, or else put on to a slate or tapestry frame.

Sewing The thread must not protrude beyond the ends of the beads.

The stitch tension should be even; if too tight the fabric will pucker, or if too loose the beads will droop and then the stitches will show.

Each bead, or group of beads, should be slipped down to the end of the thread and settled into its place before the needle is passed through the fabric to secure it.

To cover long distances, a string of beads can be laid along the pattern and secured with couching stitches. These should be made either between each bead or between small groups of three or four beads.

Cut or faceted beads are often best secured by a back stitch rather than by a continuous running stitch.

Designs Except in special circumstances beads should not be overcrowded or the effect will be clumsy and dull. If the illustrations in the text are to be used either as they stand or as a basis for pattern making, it will probably be necessary to enlarge them.

Finishing It is important that beadwork of any description should be finished off securely. To finish woven beadwork, fringes, or beads threaded on wire, pass the thread backwards through the bead next but one to the end; then through five or six more beads, and finally knot the thread and cut it off. Whenever practical the work should be stretched.

Cleaning Most bead embroidery and beadwork can be washed, spread over a soft pad, and lightly ironed. Common sense, however, must be used as some materials are unwashable and some beads unsuitable for either washing or ironing: Victorian steel beads being a case in point. Woven beadwork can be cleaned by folding it in a cloth with bicarbonate of soda, and gently shaking it so that the powder penetrates between the beads. The powder can be removed later by polishing with a soft duster or chamois leather. For very old beadwork, especially if it is frail or when sequins are involved, it is advisable to consult a specialist.

13

Part I Beads, bugles and embroidery

The first bead embroidery

EVERY time we pick up a bead on the point of a needle, pass it down the thread, and stitch it to a fabric, we are carrying out a traditional method of embroidery that was first practised long before the Ice Age.

Beads are gay, mobile, shining things—'small perforated bodies threaded for convenience with others on a string', the dictionaries describe them—and were first made far, far back in prehistory when man's needs were simple, basic and unsophisticated: a cave for shelter, a hammer, a chopper, an axe, an awl, and weapons with which to hunt his prey and his enemies. There was no place in his rigorous life for non-essentials, and yet he found time to make beads from the natural materials which surrounded him, and so perhaps they can be regarded as one of his first luxuries.

As he scuffled in the litter washed up on the seashore after a storm, among the dead branches and nuts that lay on the forest floor in autumn, or in the piles of broken stones scattered on river banks after a flood, his eyes were as quick as a beachcomber's to detect things that might be useful to him in his daily life, his hands as ready to gather them up and adapt them to his needs. So he noticed tiny, gaily coloured objects, and because they were small and intimate, they became precious to him and he used them to adorn himself in much the same casual way that a child will pick up a feather from the grass, stick it in his hair, and laugh with pleasure at the game. He saw the summer flowers and autumn berries; seeds, and slender beautifully marked shells, the frail, mottled eggs discarded from a bird's nest; and piercing them with a fishbone or a thorn, he threaded them on a straw or a length of fibre, and hung them around his neck. As simply as that the first beads were made.

1–6 Drawings from nature

15

2

3

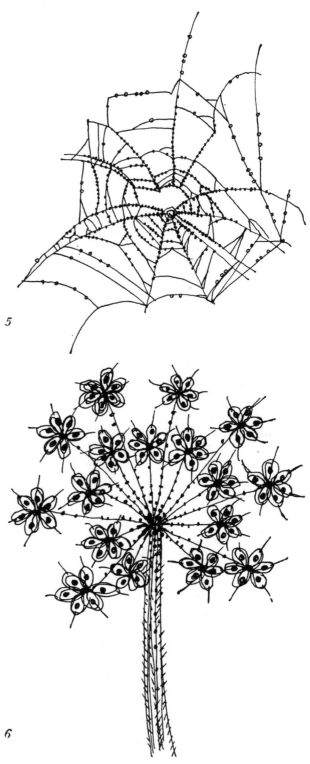

5

4

6

Because he needed nets to catch fish and snare birds, and some method by which he could attach skins to one another to make clothing, or screens to keep out the cold, he found out how to make needles and hooks from slithers of bone, and coarse threads. Some of these he cut from the hides of animals and so produced thongs; finer, stronger ones he drew from their muscles and sinews; and by rolling bark fibres between the palms of his hands or up and down along his thigh, he made a rough brown string. Given these tools and materials he was able to evolve techniques of stitching, knotting, netting and weaving, and so eventually he made the first textiles. He decorated them with shells and seeds and bits of broken bone, and bead embroidery had begun.

been made from the thin, broken bones of the small gazelles that ran wild over the country, and from the white *dentalium*, or tooth shells, that are still washed up on the beaches at the eastern end

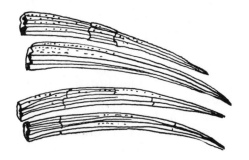

8 Dentalium shells

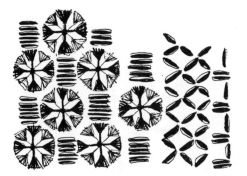

7 Seeds in combination with red and yellow surface stitchery from a wide border worked around the bottom of a tunic

Beadwork of this description was found in 1937 by some archaeologists who were excavating a group of Stone Age graves in a dry wadi on the slopes of Mount Carmel which rises steeply from the great northern plain of the modern State of Israel. As they carefully removed the dust and rubbish of so incalculably many hundreds of centuries, they saw that the skeletons still bore traces of the quite elaborately beaded head-dresses in which they had been buried, and were able to decide that they had been formed by attaching beads, in fan-shaped motifs, to some kind of net or other material. Although the net had perished and disappeared, the beads could clearly be recognised as having

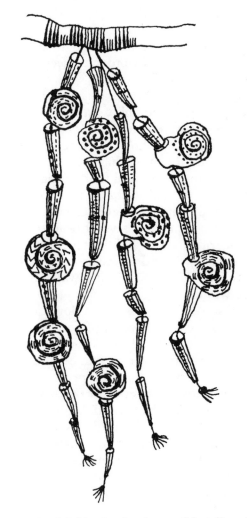

9 Part of a beaded skirt showing the use of dentalium shells

of the Mediterranean Sea today (8). These are fine, delicately ribbed shells, sickle-shaped, and closed at one end into a sharp point. It was no trouble at all for a man (or a woman) to break off the tips, between his fingers or teeth, and so create an almost inexhaustible supply of long, narrow beads, through which one or other of his threads could be passed. He did not even require equipment for boring them, as nature had already provided the holes.

However, the manufacture of primitive beads was not always just as simple as this.

When we walk along the edge of the sea, a lake or a river, we are likely to notice smooth, water-worn pebbles, and bits of coloured, stratified rock; we pick them up, find that they feel comforting in our hands and carry them with us for quite long distances, but ultimately we discard them. Early man, on the contrary, could not afford to throw anything away. He treasured the colour and the companionship of the pebbles he collected, sometimes taking them on quite long journeys; and in order to keep them safe, he turned them into beads.

Squatting on the ground, he would grasp a piece of rock between his toes, and shape it with his clumsy but efficient tools. Sometimes he would chip out the hole, working first from one side and then the other, but later he evolved the bow and pump drills and then, using some sand as an abrasive, he was able to bore the holes more rapidly and with greater ease. To polish them he would thread several beads on a string or stick, press them tightly together, and roll them backwards and forwards across a block of pumice or sandstone, pouring water over them all the while.

Because the process was slow, occupying sometimes days and weeks of constant, patient drilling and rubbing, the maker valued his beads highly, and gradually they came to be accepted as representing wealth and property, and as marks indicative of position or precedence in the family or tribe. They could be handed down from father to son, exchanged for cattle, clothing or tools, and even used to purchase a wife or a slave. Thus beads became increasingly valuable until eventually they developed into a complicated system of currency in which, for many, many centuries, much of the trade of the world was carried on.

10 Detail from a Mexican painting showing the hand drill in operation

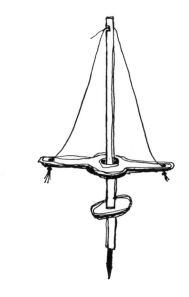

11 Pump drill

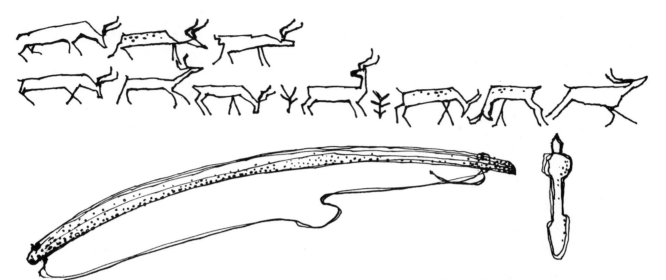

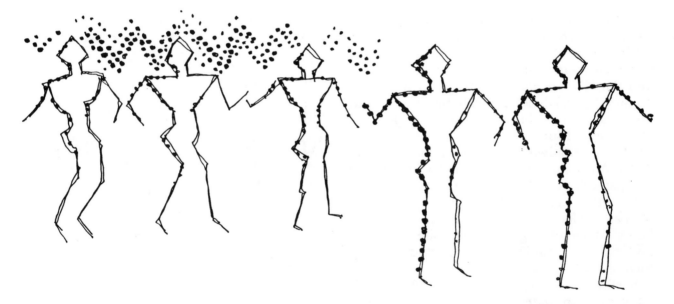

12 *Eskimo bow drill made from horn with an incised pattern of reindeer feeding*

13 *Brown bison hair bag with beaded figures, Algonquin Indians* *Pitt Rivers Museum, Oxford*

14 *Frigate birds worked in beads on a belt from the Solomon Islands*

Shell beads

BESIDES the simple, primitive shell beads which man produced by breaking and grinding, he made others out of the shell walls themselves. He fashioned them by quite complicated processes into flat discs of various sizes and degrees of thinness, bored holes through the centre, and used them both for barter and for personal adornment. Museums are full of examples of this type of beadwork. It comes from North and South America, Africa, and the Pacific Ocean; the patterns are exciting and adaptable; the beads often beautifully coloured; and anyone with an eye for detail could spend endless happy hours disentangling the intricate methods involved in threading, knotting, and weaving them.

Shell was often regarded as a sacred material. It came from water, and so in arid areas it symbolised life; when a shell was pressed to the ear the voice of the god who dwelt inside could be heard murmuring like the wind and waves; and there were not infrequently quite elaborate rites and ceremonies involved in propitiating the gods before an expedition could set out to gather shells for bead making. In March or April, for instance, when the monsoon is over and the season of the new yams has begun, the natives of the Trobriand Islands off the north-eastern tip of New Guinea, prepare themselves and their canoes to sail out into the ocean to collect the

much prized *spondylus* shells from which they make their lovely raspberry pink shell discs.

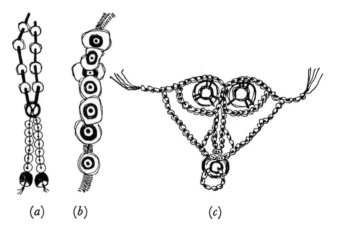

(a)   (b)   (c)

15 *Three beaded ornaments from Papua   British Museum*
(a) Pink shell discs and black plant stems threaded into a necklace
(b) Small pink shell discs laid on top of brown coconut discs, and knotted through the centre to form a band
(c) Shells threaded in the form of a face

Their acts, ritual, and time of departure are dictated by the magician of the tribe, and remote and romantic enough they sound. When he considers that a favourable period is about to commence, he gives the order to make ready the canoes. They are scraped with a specially charmed mussel shell, and provisioned for

16 *The god in the shell*

17 *Shell beads used to decorate a leather robe said to have been the habit of Pohatan, King of Virginia; which was collected in the late sixteenth or early seventeenth century, and is now in the Ashmolean Museum, Oxford*

several days, as the expedition may have to remain at sea for some time if the shells are not readily obtainable. The large hammering stones used for knocking the shells off the rocks are placed on a bed of dried banana leaves, scattered with red hibiscus flowers, and charmed over to ensure that they will hit both hard and straight; then, because the reef is far away, the magician, walking up and down upon the shore and casting his spells far out across the waves, summons the shells to move in closer; they hear his voice and respond to his call, so he now knows exactly where they will be found. The canoes sail out to an appointed meeting place and when they arrive they form into a long line, waiting while the magician meditates on some more hibiscus flowers, red croton leaves, and a few sprays of the red blossomed mangrove, thus making sure that the coloured layer within the shell walls will be bright and clear. Passing down the line of canoes he rubs the prow of each with his bunch of flowers and leaves; the men begin to paddle and so eventually the whole row evolves itself into a circle that moves slowly round the canoe

carrying the magician. The anchor stones are charmed; the water made transparent by another magic called 'sweeping the sea'; and each canoe performs some private magic. Finally a spell called 'besprinkling salt water' is uttered, and the magician gives the order for diving to begin.

Back on the coral atoll the shells are broken on a stone and each piece is rounded into a thick circular lump, slipped into a hole in a length of wood, and rubbed flat on a stone until both the outer layers have disappeared and only the lovely flat red disc remains. A hole is bored with a pump drill and a number of beads threaded on a thin, tough stick and rolled across a flat sandstone until perfectly even, cylindrical beads are produced. The women are allowed to help with the polishing, but otherwise this is an all-male activity and is typical of many of the non-European processes of bead making.

21

18 Figure drawn from mosaic for working in gold thread beads, sequins and artificial jewels   Torcello, Venice

19 Ninety-nine wooden beads separated by three spacer beads used by Mohammedans to count the names or attributes of Allah

19

Origin of the word bead

MAN has always been afraid of the unknown; and has needed something tangible to work a protective magic for him, and to turn away the sinister influence of the Evil Eye and all the other malignant forces to which he has felt himself to be exposed. To counteract them he put his faith in a handful of beads, which being small, personal, and permanent, comforted him. So he credited them with magical properties, and superstitions began to gather round them.

Their influence included his wife, his children, his property, and his cattle. A tourist in the Levantine countries today, seeing children, mules, and donkeys wearing blue beads—why blue nobody knows for certain—is witnessing the same practice still carried on.

Gradually the superstitions became attached to certain kinds of bead; amber, for instance had healing properties. The Greeks and Romans thought that a few beads made from the precious red coral of the Mediterranean would save the sailor from storm and shipwreck, the traveller from accident and ambush; in Asia they were known to repel lightning, tempests, whirlwinds, and witchcraft. In England, a string of coral beads tied quickly round the throat would stop a haemorrhage; but if the wearer was ever in danger of death they would give warning by turning pale and livid. It is not so many years since children in the East End of London wore 'bronchitis beads' to prevent them catching colds or fevers, and dire were the consequences if the beads were lost or taken off!

Far back in prehistory man used knots as a means of counting; to keep a tally of his possessions; the terms of the treaties he negotiated with his neighbours and his enemies; and of the historic events connected with his family and his tribe, its battles, victories, and heroic ancestors. It is not difficult to see how easily the knots could be replaced by beads. They were more attractive to look at; they slipped pleasantly through the fingers, and could be numbered in the dark; once again they proved themselves adaptable, useful and practical. So they found their way into religious practices, and on them men counted the prayers they offered to their gods.

This aspect of beads is of very great significance because from it we inherit our odd little word *bead*, which is peculiar to English speaking peoples and is completely unknown in other European languages.

On the continent, as is shown in the map (20), beads are commonly known as *perles*; and in the case of embroidery beads this becomes *perle de verre*, *glasperle*, and so on.

In English it comes, however, from a very old Anglo-Saxon word *bede* meaning a prayer, and so we have *bedesmen* and *bedeswomen* who lived in

NORWAY

a Perle, liten kule
b Sort perle

SWEDEN

a Pärlstav
b Stråpärla

DENMARK

a Perle, liilkugle
b Lange glasperler

GERMANY

a Perle, glasperle
b Löngliche glasperle

ENGLAND

a Embroidery bead
b Bugle bead

NETHERLANDS

a Pareltje
b Zwarte glaskraal

FRANCE

a Perle, perle de verre
b Longue perle de verre

CZECHOSLOVAKIA

a Koralek
b Skleněny korál

PORTUGAL

a Pérola
b Pérola alongada

SPAIN

a Abalorio
b Abalorios

ITALY

a Perla
b Perlina, tubetti

20 Map showing the words used in various European countries for Embroidery beads and Bugle beads

bede-houses and offered *bedes* or prayers for those whose names were recorded on the *bede-rolls* of the churches; that is to say, for people who for one reason or another were to be specially commended to the care and protection of Almighty God. The repetition of these numerous prayers had to be counted in some way—ten fingers was seldom enough—and so in the course of time the word came to be transferred from the prayers themselves to the knots or beads on which the prayers were counted.

24

Bugles

IT is obvious that if beads are to perform efficiently the function of numbering prayers from which they took their English name, they have to be easily counted by touch, and therefore they must be large rather than small, and presumably also, round in shape. But for many centuries there have been other beads made of glass which are, on the contrary, long and thin, seldom large, and never round, and these are called *bugles*, although most people, apart from embroiderers, have never heard of this term. In the trade they are referred to not simply as bugles, but as *bugle beads*; in Italian as *tubetti*; in French as *longue perle de verre* (20); but all the dictionaries agree that the etymology of this strange little English word is unknown. Bugles present themselves to us then as an interesting subject for examination, and I have tried to find out something about their origin, the purpose they served, and how they acquired their name. The evidence leads me to believe that bugles were once round as well as long; that in the beginning there was no connection whatsoever between beads and bugles, and that although alike in structure, they were put to quite different uses, neither of which had any concern with embroidery; and finally, that embroidery beads were probably once called *Lace bugle*.

Automatically and quite correctly we associate bead making with Venice, and in particular with Murano, and so, between the island and the mainland, we find during the Middle Ages, that several guilds were involved in the manufacture of a number of different kinds of bead. There were, for instance, the *cristallai*, the carvers and polishers of rock crystal, making large crystal beads that were chiefly used for rosaries and necklaces; the *perlai* who, in the secret seclusion of their glasshouses, produced *conterie*, the ordinary beads of commerce; and finally the *margaritaro*, whose work probably included the making of tiny glass beads for embroidery. Of these, the trade beads were, of course, the most important. By the time that Columbus discovered America, the Venetian glass industry was very large indeed, its prosperity being firmly established on the insatiable demands of explorers, travellers, and merchant adventurers for beads that could be exchanged for the rich natural resources of the new continents opening up around them.

But Venice was not allowed by her commercial rivals to occupy her enviable position unchallenged. In spite of stringent laws forbidding her glassmakers to work outside Italy, they were not necessarily proof against the bribes offered by other countries who were anxious to learn the secrets of their craft, and as early as 1549 the first of them arrived in London and set up a glasshouse in Crutched Friars. They soon adopted St Olave's, Hart Street, as their guild church, and their names appear quite often in the parish registers.

It has recently been shown that an enormous glass industry was established in the same way in Amsterdam and flourished there between 1608 and 1680. No doubt it supplied the needs of the Dutch East India Company, and many of the fields around Amsterdam still contain quantities of beads—the spoil and refuse of the factory—which was used at one time to manure the gardens of the rich burghers and merchants who built their houses a short distance outside the city.

By the sixteenth century, the first *betel-hutten*, or bead furnaces, were set up in Bohemia; but it was not until 1640 that an Englishman secured a patent for 'the sole Making and Venting of Beads and Beugles,' and his output was never very great. How then did the English merchants who were just as greedy for wealth and as fiercely ambitious for power as those of other nations who were all competitors in this race for overseas markets, obtain the beads they needed for trading?

The records of H.M. Customs and Excise have not, as far as I know, been studied with this special point in view, and they provide us with a great deal of entrancing information.

Customs duties existed long before 1300. The rate at which duty is charged was calculated, then as now, by reference to Rate Books, the earliest surviving example of these being dated 1550. It is surprising to find that even at this time beads were of sufficient commercial importance to attract duty, along with such nice domestic articles as *nidels*, *thymbles*, *pynnes*, and *babies for children*, which I take to mean dolls!

In the second rate book of 1604 another item appears, namely *bugle*. It is sub-headed *Great*, *Small* and *Lace*, and each of these items attracts a different rate of duty. The same entries are repeated in the next rate book which is dated 1640. Bugle, then, was something distinct from beads. The beads—made of crystal, glass, jasper, coral, and so on—were imported by the gross or by the thousand, the duty ranging from 10s. 0d. to £3; but bugle was imported by weight, and the duty on a pound of bugle was not more than 4s. 0d. and was usually much less. Bugle was clearly less valuable but was imported in far larger quantities than beads.

The import figures, which are bound in huge leather covered volumes, commence in 1696 and with only a short gap, continue until 1776. In them bugle is sometimes in the singular and sometimes in the plural, and like the rate books is classified as *Great* and *Small*; but invariably the entries are in no way connected with those for beads.

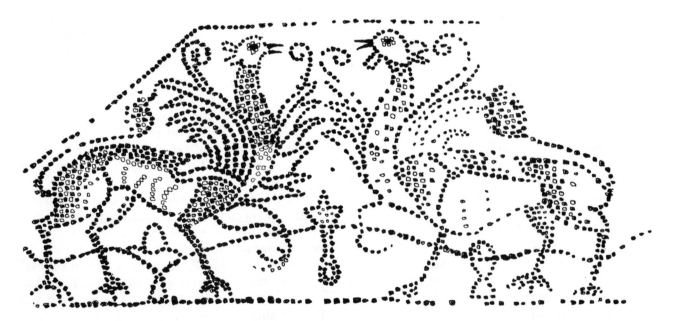

21 Mosaic on the floor of the church in Murano

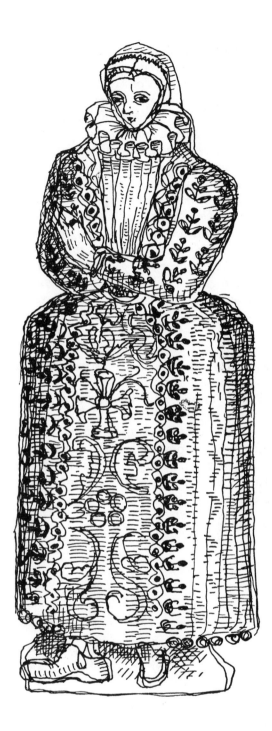

22 *Memorial brass to Jacob Verzelini, an Italian by birth, who set up a glasshouse in Crutched Friars during the sixteenth century. He and his wife are buried in the church of St Mary the Virgin, Downe, Kent. The inscription reads: Here lyeth buried . . . Jacob Verzelini Esquire borne in the Cittie of Venice, and Elizabeth his Wife, borne at Antwerpe of the ancient houses of Vanburen and Mace, who havinge lived together in Holye State of Matrimonie fortie nine years and fower moneths, departed this mortall lyfe the said Jacob the twentye day of Januarye An Dni. 1606, aged LXXXIIII years, and the said Elizabeth the XXI daye of October An Dni 1607 aged LXXIII yeares, and rest in hope of resurection to lyfe eternall*

From them we learn that both beads and bugles were procured chiefly from Germany, Holland, Italy, and Venice, though occasionally France is mentioned, and that they entered the country through the Port of London and what were known as the Out Ports, that is, at other coastal towns in southern England. If we take as an example, the period between Lady Day and Michaelmas 1697 we find that beads of *amber* and *horne* came from Germany; *corall*, *amber* and *bone*, from Holland; *black beads* from Flanders; and many *necklaces of glass* from both Venice and Holland. There were also some *glass pipes small* and some *false pearle*, but the quantities were not great and the estimated value comparatively low. On the other hand, some forty thousand pounds of Great bugles were imported at an estimated value of several thousands of pounds, and a certain amount of Small bugle. Over the years the quantities increased and the value soared.

At the end of the books one can find the export figures for the same period, and from them it is evident that by far the greater proportion of bugles were exported to Africa, to the *English Colonies* and to the *Sugar Plantations* in the West Indies, and represented business on a very large scale indeed.

Eventually the trade in bugle became so important that it was included in a special act of Parliament which received the royal assent in 1765, and was designed to facilitate the handling of certain goods that were neither manufactured in England nor intended for home consumption, but which were imported for the purpose of trading with Africa. Originally it was illegal for such goods to enter by one port and leave by another, but now the act made it lawful for the merchant to move his goods from place to place, should he find it expedient to do so. The bugles coming from Venice or Holland could thus be received in London and transferred in bond to one or other of the Out Ports, to suit the sailing of the merchant's ships or the requirements of the African importers.

Obviously, these bugles had nothing to do with embroidery, nor could they conceivably have all been long and thin. I suggest therefore that this bugle of the rate books, the import and export figures, and of the parliamentary act, was the name by which trade beads were known commercially; that they were called beads by travellers and traders as a matter of convenience; and that—if this is agreed—bugles were once of many sizes, shapes and colours and were not necessarily tube shaped.

Trade beads in East Africa

BECAUSE beads—or bugles—have been used very skilfully by native peoples for beadwork, we should know something about them from the point of view of the explorers and traders from whom they obtained them, and who, from time immemorial carried them in packs and saddle bags over rocky mountain passes, up wide swift flowing rivers, through the hot discomforts of tropical jungles, and across the aching monotony of steppes and deserts.

Year after year ton upon ton of beads was deposited in the ports of Africa, of which we will take Zanzibar as a typical example. Here in steaming, disease-haunted heat men struggled, sweated and intrigued for the rich resources of the vast hinterland of East Africa, for the rewards of commerce and for the honours of discovery. In their transactions with the natives they used beads, whose value was reckoned as second only to that of cloth and greater than that of brass or iron wire.

The situation was complicated by the fact that each kind of bead—and in 1860 it was estimated that there were about four hundred different varieties, some of which had three or four different names—had not only its own value but also its own place of preference, some tribes demanding payment for food or commodities in one colour some in another. It was a bewildering situation.

The Indian merchants of Zanzibar who would buy up a whole ship's cargo of beads, were only too willing to palm off the less popular varieties on the unwary European who, if he was a wise and cautious man, would first consult the Arab traders who travelled constantly backwards and forwards between the coast and the interior, and were therefore in a position to advise him which beads were likely to be most useful along the route that he intended to follow. Neglect in chosing beads could plunge a whole expedition into failure, financial ruin, and even into death.

When Stanley was organising his expedition to go in search of Livingstone he described his anxiety over the choice of beads as 'excrutiating' and he came to the conclusion that 'if I reckoned my requirements at fifty *khete*, or five hundred *fundo* per day, for two years, and if I purchased eleven varieties, I might consider myself safe enough.' The order was placed accordingly and he was soon able to view with pride the twenty-two sackfuls that were added to the 'comely bales and packages lying piled up, row upon row, in Capt. Webb's capacious store-room.'

The beads reached Africa loose and were then threaded on strings of palm leaf fibre and measured into three lengths the shortest of which, the *bitil*, being a single length from the tip of the index finger to the wrist; the *khete*, which would buy one day's rations for a porter,

29

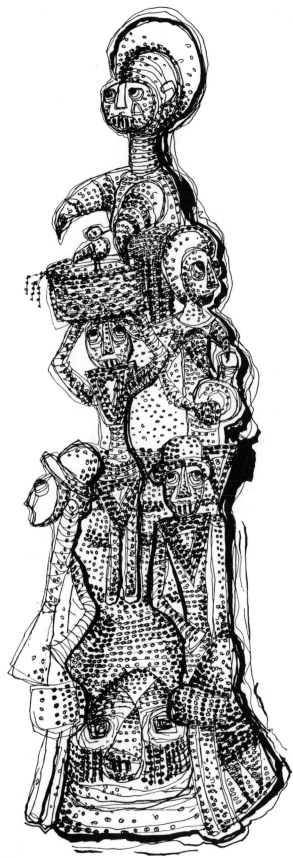

consisting of four *bitils*, that is, a double length round the thumb to the elbow, or—what is much the same—twice round the throat; and the *fundo* or *knot* composed of ten *khetes* which was used for larger purchases.

As the porters hated the inconvenience of handling boxes, beads were transported in narrow bags; matted, corded, and cradled in sticks in much the same way as cloth. Loading the porters required both skill and experience especially if, like beads, the load would decrease towards the end of the journey.

The cheapest beads which formed the staple of commerce in East Africa were called *hafizi*. They were coarse porcelain beads, usually white but available also in brick red or bright yellow. We are all familiar with these white beads which are the mainstay of much of the beadwork of Africa and North America.

The most expensive beads were coral red in colour and were called *sam-sam*, *samé-samé*, or *sami-sami*. The Africans were so ravished by them that they were known also as *kimara-p'hamba*, or food-finishers, because a man would part with his dinner to obtain them; and as *kifunjya-niji*, or town breakers, because the women were willing to ruin themselves and their husbands in order to become possessed of a few *khete* of them.

Other local names included *gulabi* (rosy); *mzizima* a few strings of which were required to close the bargain when slaves were being purchased; *sungomaji* which were useful for buying ivory and which in certain places could be used to pay for the hire of boats; *bubu*, a black Venetian bead that came in fourteen sizes; *sofi*, called in Italian *cannetone*; *nili* meaning coconut leaves because they were made of transparent green glass; *lungenya*, a coarse red porcelain bead.

But beadwork of even the most ardent mission schools could hardly have absorbed more than a fraction of the quantities imported. They were by no means perishable, and although the East

23 In Nigeria there is a two-hundred-year-old tradition of beadwork among the Yoruba, who create fantastic erections that become part of the royal regalia and are used during coronation ceremonies British Museum

African carried his wealth upon his person, only about a third wore beads in any quantity, and often seemed to weary quite soon of the *khetes* that only a short time before they had been eager to acquire in exchange for goats, corn, and other foodstuffs. Where then did they go?

The question may, in part, be answered by a story told by Stanley in *How I found Livingstone*.

Arriving one day at the northern stream of the Rugufu river he says that he distinctly heard a sound like thunder in the west, and upon asking what it was he was told that 'there is a great mountain on the other side of (Lake) Tanganyika, full of deep holes in which the water rolls; when there is a wind on the Tanganyika there is a sound like *mvuha* (thunder). Many boats have been lost there, and it is the custom with Arabs and natives to throw cloth and beads, and especially white beads, to appease the *mulunga* (god) of the lake. Those who throw beads generally get past without trouble, but those who do not throw beads get lost and drowned.'

I understand that every year thousands of beads, of all ages, are washed up on the beaches and islands on the east coast of Africa. Some no doubt, like those that the tide casts up on the shores of St Agnes in the Scillys, from suspected wrecks that occurred amongst the vessels bound for the Canaries and North America, but others perhaps offered to appease the fury of a vengeful deity. In this way the lakes, rivers, and streams of Africa may have received large quantities of beads the disappearance of which has never been satisfactorily accounted for.

Stuart beadwork

LONG before needlewomen of the nineteenth century discovered the possibilities of beadwork, comparatively coarse beads had been used in various parts of Europe for embroidery for a very long time indeed. A great deal of work was done, for example, during the thirteenth and fourteenth centuries in Lower Saxony, examples of which can be seen in Hanover and Darmstadt. The beads were usually attached to vellum, and it has been suggested that the existence of this beadwork might—like the German whitework or *opus Teutonicum* of the Middle Ages—be interpreted as a sign of poverty amongst the German convents at this time, and that the beads were perhaps a substitute for work in pearls, precious metals, and the coveted Byzantine enamels. Nevertheless, the vestments and hangings must have gleamed with considerable beauty in the dark, candle lit cathedrals and churches, shining through the dimness like the stained glass in the windows, and there seems little doubt that the designs were good and well drawn.

In Spain, too, examples of very old beading are not unknown, and a beaded cap was recovered from the tomb of Ferdinand de la Certe who was buried in Las Huelgas, near Burgos, in 1275. It is worked in blue glass beads, seed pearls, and coral beads on a linen material which was then stretched over a framework of wood and bound around the edges with gold foil. Rampant lions and double headed eagles cover the cap on a chequered background. Like the head-dresses from Mount Carmel, the cap must have been considered of some value, or it would not have been used for burial.

Stuart beadwork has often much the same character and qualities as this earlier embroidery, and at first sight it looks coarse and unlovely by comparison with the elegant silk and gold needlework of the period. The designs are usually those used for embroidery but the beads sharpen their outlines and make them engagingly irrational, and they are, of course, a valuable source of design material.

As the combination of beads with wire is a particularly sturdy one, a good many baskets, trays and table ornaments still exist, as well as the mirror frames, pictures and caskets that were worked on the familiar satin with its unmistakable green selvedges. But where did the Stuarts suddenly discover these harsh, garishly coloured little beads? Who first thought of using them in this outlandish manner, so unlike anything that one would have expected to flourish in the climate of contemporary taste? Who or what inspired the craze that erupted so suddenly about 1630, flourished for a season, and finally died out some fifty years later coinciding almost exactly with the years during which trade beads were being manufactured in great

24 Head in blue beads and coral. South Germany
Victoria and Albert Museum

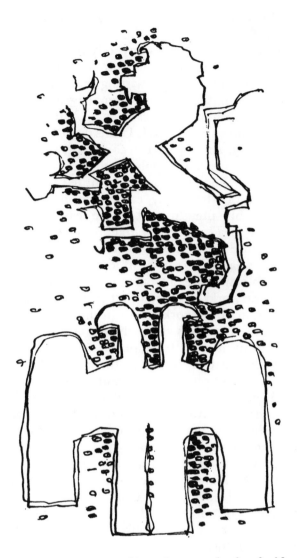

26 Detail of design on thirteenth-century bead embroidered
cap   Las Huelgas, Burgos

25 Bead embroidery on parchment, late thirteenth century
Lower Saxony Cathedral Museum, Halberstadt
Drawn from 'The Art of Embroidery' 1964

25

numbers in the factory in Amsterdam, and imported from there by the London merchants.

It is hardly likely that anybody thought, 'Ah, let us make beads which will be suitable for pictures or trays, or for twisting into baskets on awkward lengths of strong unmanageable wire, or for this fashionable *Embost* or *on the stamp work* that we know as *stumpwork*. Crafts do not develop in this way. An object or a commodity is there, usually in plentiful supply, and one day somebody says: 'Look at those queer little beads that are used for—let us say, commerce. Beads they may be, but they are not in the least like embroidery beads, nor yet like those on which prayers are counted or necklaces threaded. Can they be adapted to satisfy, at least for a time, the insatiable appetite of women for something new to sew or work?' I suggest that it is very possible that Stuart beadwork began in much this way, and that the beads themselves may have been some form of small trade beads.

In the British Museum there is a box of traveller's samples of trade beads dated 1704. It consists of seven trays to which rows of beads are attached. The trays are bound together to form a cumbersome but quite portable book, measuring fifteen by nine inches, and six inches in depth. Some of the beads are enormous and many are known to have been used for the purchase of slaves, gum, gold, and ivory; some are made of porcelain, delicately painted, and others are made of coloured glass. They are similar to those used for beading a vase and stand made in South Germany *c.* 1730, and now in the Victoria and Albert Museum (46); but the smallest glass beads in the box are even more interesting because they are so like the coarser of the beads on Stuart beadwork.

Here we must, however, enter realms of pure fantasy. Somebody—a quick witted haberdasher perhaps—seeing a chance to increase his business if he could devise some way of using this readily available and inexpensive commodity, may have been struck with the bright idea of selling the smallest of the trade beads for working the ready traced embroidery patterns he always kept in stock, instead of the usual silks and wools he habitually sold and recommended. Perhaps he also saw that they could be used to make, by an ingenious threading process, little *swete bagges* for holding herbs or lavender, or alms for

distribution to the poor. A haberdasher sold wires, too, of various kinds, and it is not difficult to see him combining beads with wire to make strong baskets, trays and ornaments. Then there were on his shelves, besides all this, the stamped cards on which the puppet like characters of the *stamp* or *stumpwork* world were constructed, and these were as easily dressed in beads as in lace and materials. He had only to buy up a few beads, see how the novelty took on, and there might be considerable profit for him. He may even have called it *buglework*.

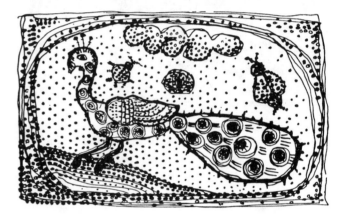

27 *Peacock worked in beads and surface stitchery, late seventeenth century*

In the possession of Miss J. Weatherhead

28 *Traveller's sample box of trade beads 1704*

British Museum

34

29 *Brushwork patterns on trade beads, contained in the sample box. They could be used for small beaded patterns*

30 *'Moths, fruicts, flowers and insects' from a beaded picture, c. 1680*
Lady Lever Gallery, Port Sunlight

31

32

31–2 Bottom and one side of a Stuart beaded basket
Fitzwilliam Museum, Cambridge

33 Raised beadwork picture, c. 1680
Lady Lever Gallery, Port Sunlight

Lace bugle

IF Great and Small bugles were trade beads, what then was Lace bugle, the third type of bugle listed in the rate books, and appearing occasionally in the import figures?

It was, I believe, the name by which embroidery beads as opposed to buglework beads, were originally known in England, a conclusion that has been reached by studying the beads themselves and by considering two definitions in a very old dictionary.

In 1610 an interesting character called John Florio published an Italian-English dictionary called *Queen Anna's World of Words*. He was a very able man, the son of an Italian protestant who fled to England during the reign of Edward VI to escape persecution. (It is worth while recalling that at the same period the first Venetian glassmakers were also on their way to London.) In 1581 Florio, who was completely bilingual, matriculated at Magdalen College, Oxford, where he became known as a tutor and instructor of certain scholars in the university. His ability as a writer and teacher attracted the attention of the man who was Shakespeare's own patron—the Earl of Southampton—who, in Florio's own words, took him 'into his pay and patronage'. In this way he became personally acquainted with the great literary figures of his day, and gathered such a reputation to himself that in 1603 he was appointed reader in Italian

to Queen Anne, the wife of James I; so he called his great dictionary after his royal pupil, and dedicated it to his patrons, the Earl of Southampton and the Earl and Countess of Rutland.

Florio gives two definitions which throw an altogether new and different light on the origin of bugles. He tells us that in Italian—as in Latin—a pearl is translated *margarita*. But to this he adds two other words, *margaritine* and *margaritaro*. The first he defines as 'seed-pearles or bugles', and the second as 'one that pierceth or boreth pearls, a maker of bugles'.

Seed pearls are extremely small; a man who pierces or bores them is accustomed to working with a magnifying glass and the most delicate tools, so it is more than likely that the bugles he is said to make will also be small and quite unlike the bugles used for trade and we know from the evidence of an eighteenth-century manuscript in the Correr Museum, Venice, that the *margaritaro* made them by chopping up long thin tubes or *canes* of glass (34); and this method of bead making was totally different from that being practised by the *perlai* in the same manuscript who sits by her bellows making trade beads by catching the drops as they melt from the solid glass rod that she holds in the flame that burns on her bench (35).

One of the New Year gifts received by Queen Elizabeth in 1600 was 'a mantle of black silk

34 *Margaritaro at work chopping glass 'canes' into beads
From an eighteenth-century manuscript, 'Correr Museum',
Venice*

35 *Perlai at work; drawn from a Venetian manuscript of the
eighteenth century*

35

clothe edged with a fine bone lace of small pearle and bugle'. This shows us that bugle was not just another name for seed pearls; that it was either black or suitable for wearing with black; and that it was light enough to be combined with lace.

In the collection of lace in the Victoria and Albert Museum there is a fragment of Venetian *punto in aria* of the late sixteenth or early seventeenth century. A dragon with a curving tail and two birds with widespread wings survive among its tattered edges, and each has a minute black bead marking its eye. Unless you are looking for them they are almost invisible. There is also a small picture in English needlepoint lace of the same period in which seed pearls and the same fine black beads have been used together. The subject is the *Judgment of Solomon*; the pearls enrich the clothing of the figures and the canopy under which Solomon sits, and the holes left in the lace for the eyes of both the figures and the insects that form, as one would expect, a background decoration, have been filled in with minute black glass beads. Perhaps they were called *lace bugle*.

Very slightly larger beads can also be found set between two pieces of silver gilt thread to mark the eyes on the animals, birds, and insects that were worked—possibly by Mary Queen of Scots—on some unrestored embroideries at Hardwick Hall, Derbyshire. These are, it is believed, the earliest surviving examples of the use of beads for embroidery by Englishwomen.

Dr Johnson, in his dictionary of 1775 defines bugle as 'a shining bead of black glass', and gives as an illustration a quotation from one of the Shakespearean sonnets:

'Tis not your inky brows, your black silk hair,
Your bugle eyeballs, or your cheek of cream
That can entame my spirits to your worship.

It is doubtful whether any man ever thought of the eyes of his beloved as being like tube shaped beads, but it would have been entirely possible for him to have compared them to the 'shining beads of black glass' which he saw her wearing combined with seed pearls in the lace at her throat, or working into the eyes of the creatures she stitched on her embroidery frame.

39

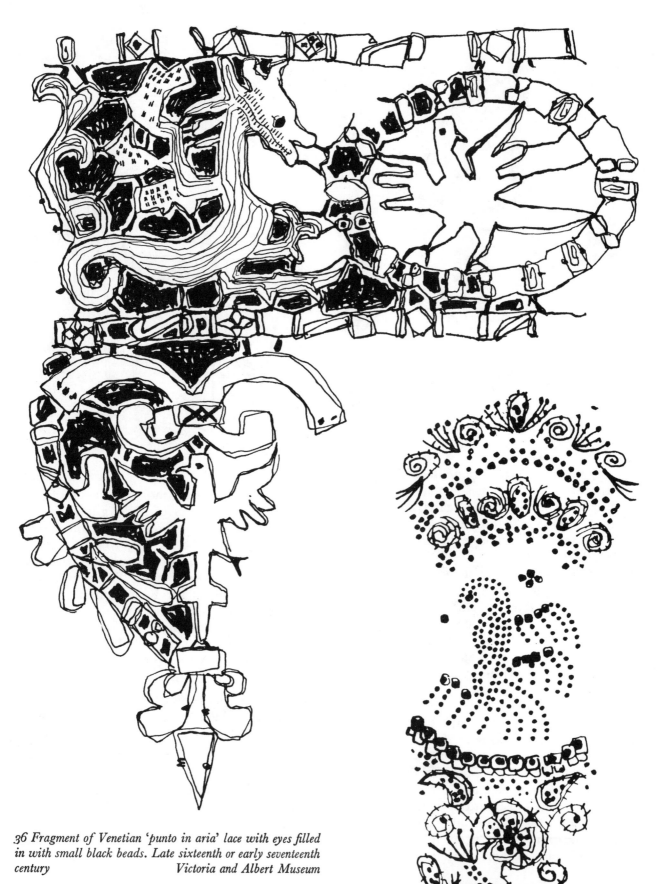

*36 Fragment of Venetian 'punto in aria' lace with eyes filled
in with small black beads. Late sixteenth or early seventeenth
century   Victoria and Albert Museum*

40

37

38 'The Judgement of Solomon'. English needlepoint lace with seed pearls and small black beads. Late sixteenth or early seventeenth century   *Victoria and Albert Museum*

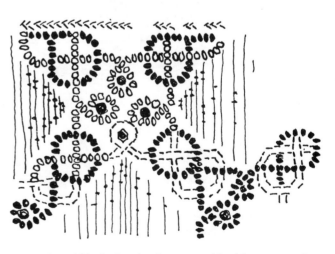

37 Opposite: '*The Pelican in her piety*', her eye marked by a tiny black bead. Elizabethan glove
Guildhall Museum, London

39 Pearls and black glass beads were combined in a geometric pattern on her sampler by Jane Bostocke in 1598
Victoria and Albert Museum

40 *Detail from a chair-back, showing the use of beads for eyes*   *Hardwick Hall, Derbyshire*

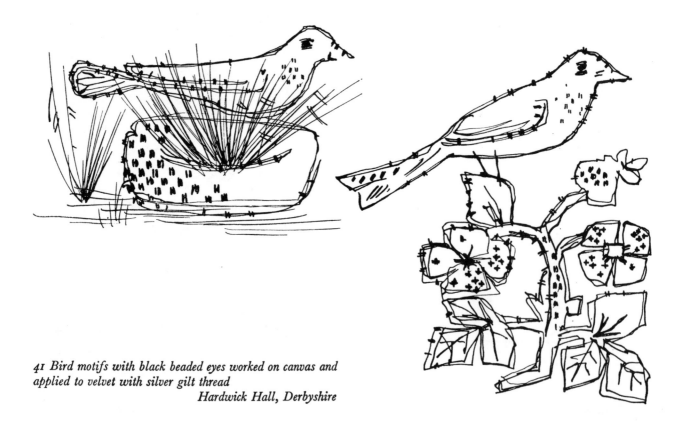

41 *Bird motifs with black beaded eyes worked on canvas and applied to velvet with silver gilt thread*
                    Hardwick Hall, Derbyshire

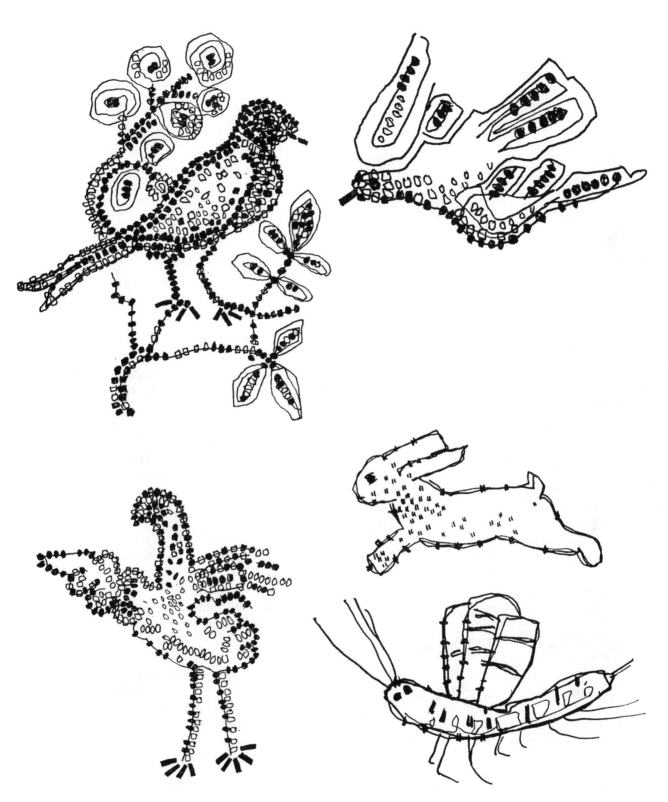

42 *Birds from a seventeenth-century picture, showing the use
of black bugle beads for feet and beaks*
Fitzwilliam Museum, Cambridge

43 *Rabbit and butterfly with beaded eyes on a velvet bedspread*
Hardwick Hall, Derbyshire

Buglework

THE first English reference to buglework appeared in 1710 when an *Advertisement* was printed in No. 245 of *The Tatler* which purported to have been received from a certain Lady Fardingale who claimed to have been robbed of various possessions by her maid Bridget Howd'ee. The maid is accused of carrying off 'with the help of her consorts' such fascinating articles as 'bracelets of braided hair, Pomander, and Seed-Pearl'; 'one silver gilt (box) of a large size for Cashu and Carraway Comfits, to be taken at long Sermons'; and an embroidered picture of

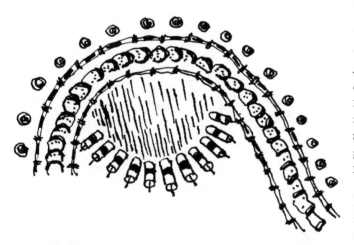

44 *Detail of embroidery on a sleeve (Italian?), late sixteenth or early seventeenth century, showing bugle beads held in place with surface stitches Victoria and Albert Museum*

'Adam and Eve in Bugle-Work, without Fig Leaves, upon Canvas, curiously wrought by Her Ladyship's own Hand'.

Bugle beads in the modern sense were used during the late sixteenth and early seventeenth centuries for embroidery. They can be seen on a pair of handsome green silk sleeves in the Victoria and Albert Museum, which are thought to be of Italian workmanship and to date from this period. Each bead is held in place not only through the pipe, but also by two or three stitches that have been worked across the centre of the tube.

They were also used by the French embroiderers who called them *jais*. In 1770 they were described by Saint-Aubin in *L'Art du Brodeur* as '*verre fondu et file en petits tubes de toutes coleurs*'; and to this he adds the interesting footnote: '*Le jais de Milan est plus egal de grosseur et mieux coupe.*' Amongst his illustrations is one showing how bugle beads can be stitched together in rows with a little tag or tassel suspended from them.

So glass bugle beads were readily available to Lady Fardingale, and she knew that the thread she sewed them with should be waxed because, according again to Saint-Aubin, this was common practice at the time. '*Pour l'employer en broderie, on l'enfile de laiton ou de soie bien cirée le coudre sur l'etoffe,*' he says.

Although few examples exist, bugle beads were, at precisely this time, used in combination with surface stitchery, in an entirely different manner and to create a very unusual effect.

One of these rare embroideries in the form of a dossal, is still hanging in the church in Weston Favell, Northamptonshire, for which it was originally made. On it is depicted a lively version of the Last Supper (45). The table is laid with cutlery, dishes, and candles; the salt cellar is beside Judas whose hand clutches the money-bag; two servants stand by with the ewer and basin for washing the feet; there are two more candles in sconces on the wall; two overhanging curtains caught up with three large bows; and below are the words *Weston Favell 1697*. The figures are worked in silk surface stitchery and metal threads, and the entire background is covered with glass bugle beads sewn in long vertical rows.

Bugle beads also cover the backgrounds of a series of wall hangings that have been in the private apartments at Knebworth House for a considerable period of time. In this case the patterns are floral and the bugles are threaded on very fine wire and couched in concentric circles to fit into the spaces between the branches, flowers, leaves, and fruit. Whether the beads are contemporaneous with the embroidery, we do not know; nor has the work been dated.

Sufficient bugle beads to cover a large background weigh a considerable amount. The threads securing them to the fabric would easily rub and break, especially if—as in both these examples—the embroidery was designed to be hung, and therefore it is not surprising that so little remains of what may once have been quite a big corpus of work. At the same time, it is unlikely that the method was used for anything except hangings as the whole object must have been to achieve the softly luminous and almost silky sheen that makes the dossal and the floral hangings glow and shimmer. Laid flat, there is little to commend the work at all, as the backgrounds, receiving no direct light, remain cold and glassy, metallic and dull. Whether or not this was also called Bugle Work we have at present no means of knowing.

46 Motifs from 'a vase and stand encrusted with Venetian beadwork'. German, c. 1730   Victoria and Albert Museum

47 'Adam and Eve and the subtil serpent'. Drawn from a
photograph of the embroidery on an altar cloth dated 1651
Hungarian National Museum, Budapest

48 Part of the pattern on an eighteenth-century apron; the
petals and leaves are sewn rather irregularly with bugle beads
In the possession of Mrs C. Williams

Spangles, sequins and artificial jewels

THE thin, flat, brightly shining discs with a small hole in the centre that we call sequins, had originally no more to do with embroidery than had beads themselves, being the name of some golden coins that were minted in Venice, Milan, and Genoa during the thirteenth century.

Like beads, sequins have a trade name and are known commercially as *paillettes*; or, if the disc is slightly concave as *couvettes*.

If, however, the hole is not in the centre but towards one side, so that the disc is suspended like a pendant, it is officially called a sequin. If there are two holes placed opposite each other on the circumference of this disc, or if it is ringed with holes, it is a sequin; and finally, if it is oval shaped and has a hole at each end, it is still a sequin.

But these classifications are comparatively modern and as far as I can discover the word sequin was not in common use in connection with embroidery before the middle of the nineteenth century.

To Diderot, in his great *Receuil de Planches sur les Sciences et les Arts* of 1763, they were all *paillettes*, and the illustration he provides under the heading of *Brodeur* shows us two women at work in a well-lit room, one pointing out the way in which she has dressed her frame and transferred the design to the fabric stretched on it, and the other seated already behind her frame, surrounded by the scissors, pins, needles, and other tools of her craft. These include a shallow dish and what is presumably a circular pad of material on which she has placed some tiny objects that might be assumed to be beads, pearls, or gold chips, but the detailed drawings below show us clearly that they are what we would today call sequins. Those in the dish are round, oval and heart shaped, and each is surrounded by a ring of holes; two different methods of attaching them by means of gold chips are illustrated, and the group is labelled *Paillettes de differentes formes*; *paillettes rondes, grandes et moyennes*; *paillettes ovales*, and *paillettes en coeur*. The others, scattered for convenience on the pad, are round flat discs with a central hole and are graded in seven sizes. They are captioned *petites paillettes*, and to the smallest a special note is attached, namely, *on nomme semence celle de la plus petite espece*. These paillettes are also shown stitched together in an overlapping row, and the note on this reads *Cette façon de les coudre fait qu'on les nomme paillettes comptées*.

In all this the word 'sequin' simply does not occur.

During the latter part of the Elizabethan period and in the reign of James I and Charles I, small eyelets called *oes* were much used for trimming bodices, foreparts, gowns, petticoats, doublets and accessories, and also for theatrical

48

49 *Different types of paillettes used during the eighteenth century*
From D. Diderot, 'L'Encyclopedie raisonne des sciences, des arts et des metiers' Vol. II (1762)

50 *Sequin-scattered background and border on a mid-seventeenth-century panel   Bethnal Green Museum, London*

costume. Like spangles, with which they were often linked in contemporary records, they were chiefly made of gold and copper, and became fashionable about 1575 when a certain Robert Sharp was granted a patent to manufacture 'spangles and oes of gold'. These he must have sold for about six shillings an ounce as this was the price paid for them by Lord Howard of Naworth in 1616. At approximately the same date the duty levied on 'spangles of copper, the thousand', amounted to one shilling. The Tudors, of course, lavished spangles on their embroideries, and among the New Year gifts received by the Queen in 1577 were 'two littil vales set wih spangills'; 'a dublet of white networke floushed al over with silver spangills'; and 'three pieces of networke with spangills and threads of gold'; and in 1600 she had 'a loose gowne of ladie-blush satten, laide with a bone-lace of Venice golde and silver, with spangles.'

Like sequins, artificial jewels are admissable in all sorts of bead embroidery. They are of many kinds, the majority being cut to look exactly like real gems, and are backed with foil for greater brilliance. Some are mounted on gilt claws, but if unset they are pierced with tiny holes through which it is often none too easy to pass the smallest needle. When this difficulty arises it can sometimes be overcome by passing the thread itself through the hole, just as though it was the eye of a needle; the needle must then be re-threaded, and the jewel stitched in place. The stitches should be made as closely as possible to the edge of the jewel, and two or three in each hole is usually sufficient as jewelled embroidery is not, on the whole, subject to hard wear. The material must of course be framed and the thread waxed. At least one encircling piece of gold

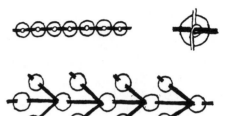

51 Small, medium and large sequins attached in three different ways

52 Elaborate gold embroidery with sequins from the design traditionally worked on the red velvet dresses worn by one hundred 'demoiselles d'honneur' at the Russian Imperial court. Late eighteenth century

In the possession of Lady Zia Wernher

50

thread can be laid around each jewel, the ends of which must be pushed through to the wrong side in the usual way, and not hidden—as is very tempting—underneath the stone as this will prevent it from lying flat. If other rows are to be added, as is occasionally the case in ecclesiastical embroidery, much of the success of the whole setting will depend on the careful sewing of this first round. Care should be taken that the rings are exactly even and the gold thread fastened off precisely in line with the place at which it began or the number will be uneven. It is as well to make the setting no wider than the diameter of the stone or it will be too heavy and the colour of the jewel overwhelmed.

If the stone is square, a short straight length of purl can be placed along each side with good effect; or alternatively a neat piece of purl or a bead stitched over each hole in the jewel, or a string of tiny beads couched around its edge. This looks well on jewels of any shape. But whatever you decide to do will depend on the effect you are striving to create, whether it is for the star-dust airiness of jewelled and spangled net, the elaborate richness of formal evening dress, or the barbaric splendours one associates with operatic arias and the extravagance of theatrical costume. Only remember that if the jewels are to be on semi-transparent material they must be stitched individually, and the thread begun and ended afresh each time, otherwise it will spoil the look of the embroidery by being visible on the wrong side.

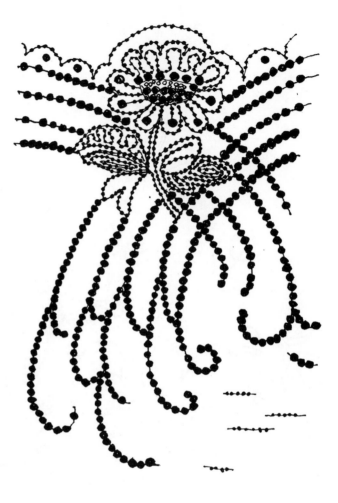

53 Late nineteenth-century commercial design with sequins with beads on net

54 *Large beaded panel in pinks and mauve from a black sequin covered dress 1920*   *Victoria and Albert Museum*

On buying beads

TODAY we buy beads in plastic bags and boxes, less frequently in bunches. How were they sold in, say, Victorian times? where did Tudor and Stuart women buy them? how were they distributed about the country? were they sold by hundreds, by thousands, or by weight? and having acquired them, how were they stored?

Beads, like 'bobbing lace' and pins were probably sold by pedlars 'att the gate' of the great houses, and by stallholders in fairs and street markets. In the collection of toys in the Bethnal Green Museum, London, there are several period dolls dressed as both pedlars and fairground women, and beads are included in the stocks of tiny lightweight wares they offer to their customers.

They would have obtained them in the first place from the haberdashers who supplied goods both wholesale and retail, and whose trade cards often include beads amongst their entrancing stock of baskets, pin-cushions, chimney lines, points and laces, gloves, ribbons, quilted bed gowns, stomachers and shapes, child bed linen, and 'cradles fitted in the neatest manner'. In 1755 for example, Robert Bright, haberdasher, at the Golden Fleece and Glove, Cheapside, advertised 'French and Bugle of all sorts'; a year later Goodyar's and Houlden's warehouse at the Golden Heart on the corner of Duke Street and Piccadilly, sold 'a large assortment of French

beads'; and Teasdale and Squibb were willing to sell 'English and French beads' to the ladies in Bath or London.

55 *Pedlar doll from Portsmouth with beads, rosaries and bugle beads on his tray 1810*　*Bethnal Green Museum, London*

53

56 *Pedlar doll with beads, frames and wools in her basket*
Bethnal Green Museum, London

57 *Storage bottles used for beads   Castle Museum, York*
Linen bag containing beads a loop of which is stitched to the
side   Gawthorpe Foundation, Burnley, Lancs.
Various small boxes used for beads
Platt Hall Museum, Manchester, and Embroiders' Guild,
London

57

The large, cylindrical beads were known as 'O.P.' beads and were first imported about the middle of the century from Germany; but the little seed shaped beads which were usually sold by weight, were called 'pound beads'. These came in three sizes: a fine, almost minute bead, used for loom work and netting purses, bracelets and neck chains; No. 2, the middle size, for canvas work; and the largest, No. 3, was considered suitable for crocheted borders and heavy furnishing fringes.

Some were also, of course, sold in bunches, but perhaps the oddest sidelight on this minikin of a subject comes curiously enough, from the other side of the world. In New Zealand, until very recently beads were sold by the thimbleful. The price was one shilling and it was said to take eight or nine thimblefuls to bead a dress.

Advice in chosing beads was a favourite subject with nineteenth-century editors. In 1855 Godey was telling the American readers of his *Lady's Book* that 'enough beads for the work to be undertaken, should be purchased at once, as it is seldom that they can be accurately matched, either as regards shade, hue, size or pattern. In bugles, too, there is much trickery, especially in the black ones; they must always be purchased with reference to their use, and then an even, smooth, bright looking bugle chosen—not too fine in the pipe, or it will be difficult to work them'.

54

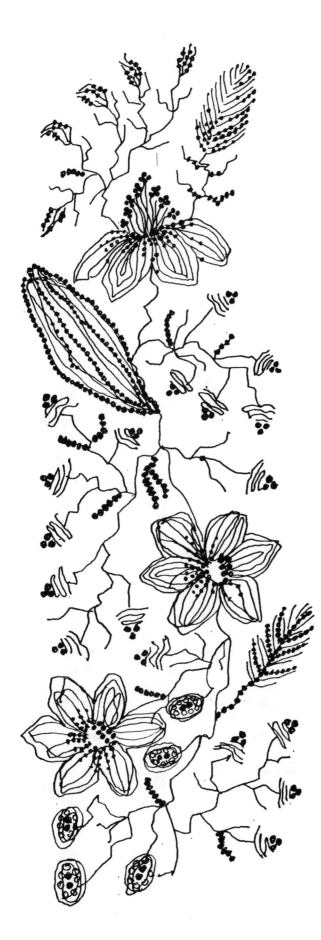

58 Typical early Victorian beaded patterns on velvet

Needlewomen are frugal creatures, treasuring scraps of material, ends of silks, odd buttons, shreds of this and that for which an urgent use may one day be found. Miss Florence Hartley writing in her *Ladies' Hand Book* in 1859 suggests that 'where coloured glass beads are used, it is better to arrange them in separate bags, with the color written on the outside of the bag', but examination of many old workboxes shows that, as might be expected, there has never been a system, only a more or less personal muddle, and that beads have always gone into the first little container that comes to hand.

Pearl embroidery

IN one sense our bright little glass beads in their plastic containers are rather an unfortunate substitute for the pearls which were once liberally used for embroidery. There are many references to them in household accounts and inventories, descriptions of special dresses and trimmings on which they were used, even the exact number being sometimes recorded; and yet most of us know little or nothing about them, beyond the fact that Florio's *margaritaro* made holes in them. How did he, we might wonder, pierce so frail and tiny an object? and where did his supplies come from? Why are pearls not listed in the customs figures?

They were not as one might suppose, obtained from the pearl oyster of the warm, tropical seas, but from a small freshwater mollusc with a thick, coarse shell, that is widely distributed in the rivers, lakes, and streams of almost every continent. They are found from Siberia to the Himalayas, and in the majority of European rivers; there have been pearl fisheries for thousands of years on the rivers of China, especially in Manchuria; bushels of them have been recovered from ancient burial mounds in the Mississippi Valley; and although they do not occur in the Midlands and in south-east England they were once plentiful in Cornish streams, in Wales, Yorkshire, and Scotland; in the Shetlands, the Isle of Man, and in many parts of Ireland.

In fact the Venerable Bede as early as the seventh century, includes them in his list of things for which Britain had long been famous.

The principal pearl-bearing mollusc of Europe is *Unio margaritifera*; in France it is known as *moule* or *huître perlière*; in Germany as *perlenmuschel*; in Russia as *schemtschwschuaja rakavina*; and in English we call them simply *pearl mussels*. William Camden, the historian, who was a contemporary of Florio, tells us that in Ireland they were called *Kregin Diliw* or Deluge Pearls, on the assumption that they were carried there by the biblical flood. He also adds that those who fish for pearls know partly by the outsides of the muscles whether they contain any; for such as have them are generally a little distorted from their usual shape. No special skill was, in fact, required by the peasant fishermen, only good eyesight and a capacity to wade about in cold water for long hours. However, fishing usually took place when the water was low during July and August when, as a proclamation of the Privy Council of Scotland put the matter in 1621, 'they are at their chief perfection'.

Many pearls were of course large and very valuable, but the small, often misshapen or discoloured ones concern us, and were undoubtedly those used for embroidery. As many as twelve were often found in one shell, though greater but

59 *A large proportion of the pearls that once enriched the 'opus anglicanum' have disappeared but sometimes the figures retain their pearl outlines*

60 *Drawing from an old print showing pearl fishers at work in a river. To collect the molluscs they carried tongs or long sticks which were thrust into the shells when open; many fishers used their toes*

perhaps apocryphal numbers have been reported. The important thing is that not only was there from an early time a demand for these small pearls but also that there were abundant local supplies which were only exhausted as another writer puts it 'through avarice of the undertakers'. To give some idea of the scale of the industry it is interesting to note that between 1761 and 1764 ten thousand pounds worth of pearls reached the London markets from Scotland alone, and were sold from 10s. 0d. to £1 6s. 0d. per ounce.

It was a fluctuating industry and seems to have received its last impetus as late as 1861, when a German merchant, travelling in the Scottish districts of Tay, Doon, and Don, discovered that many country people, who at that time were very poor indeed, possessed small hoards of pearls. So little did they think of them that they were astonished when they found that he was willing to purchase them, and forthwith it seemed that every man, woman and child, the able-bodied, the aged, the infirm, and the young, took to searching the rivers once more for pearls. In a wonderfully short time the merchant had accumulated a collection whose richness and variety can seldom have been surpassed. The

trade developed rapidly, pearls became fashionable, more particularly perhaps because Queen Victoria approved all things Scottish, and so we find both dress and embroidery of the period sewn over with pearls.

Inside their calcareous shells pearls are soft as butter, and one of the major difficulties in piercing them is to work the drill so that it emerges precisely opposite its point of entry. If they are valuable they are usually bored first from one side and then from the other, but it is unlikely that the inferior pearls used for embroidery was treated with any such special care. The *margaritaro* and his fellow craftsmen employed in this small but specialised field, probably worked with the same bow drill as that developed and used by the first beadmakers to bore holes in shells and pebbles. It is still in use today, and I am told that it would have been entirely possible for a craftsman of any period to pierce the most minute pearl with the bow drill. Either he would have taken each pearl individually between the fingers of his left hand and operated the drill with his right or else to have set the pearls in wax—and I understand that up to fifty pearls could be set at once—and pierced them, as it were, in bulk.

61

63

62

64 (a)

61 *Example to show how frugally pearls were used during the seventeenth century. The central figure on this embroidered cushion cover was worked during the reign of Charles II and although she has been given—or has given herself—a pearl necklace, they are used nowhere else in the design*
Bethnal Green Museum, London

62 *Wooden bowl with handle for holding wax in which pearls and other jewels are set while being pierced or worked*
Drawn in a jeweller's workroom Ponte Vecchio, Florence

63 *Pearl and gold embroidery on a coif; early seventeenth century*
Victoria and Albert Museum

58

64 Two figures from a triptych—St Sebastian and St Ursula—in 'reliefstickerei' or raised work. The robes are covered with tiny golden 'paillettes semences' and the folds outlined in pearls. It is thought to have been made in Nurnberg about 1519. Compare with (a) a similar piece of embroidery in the Treasury of Trogir Cathedral, Yugoslavia, in which St Martin is giving his cloak to the beggar

In the Bavarian State Museum, Munich

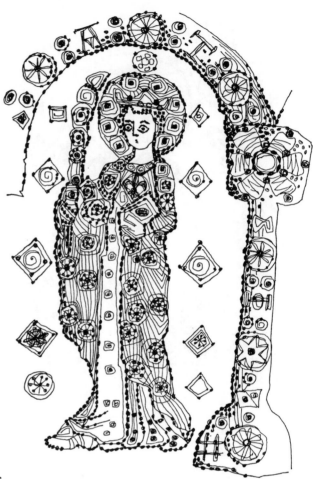

65

67

66

65 'The Angel of the Annunciation' with halo outlined in carefully gradated pearls, sixteenth century
Byzantine Museum, Athens

66 The Vestments of the Golden Fleece were heavily embroidered in pearls; the illustration shows part of the pattern
From a cope Hofburg Museum, Vienna

67 Metal plates and pearls on one of the figures on an altar frontal at Cheb, Austria   *Drawn from a photograph*

Russian pearl embroidery

PERHAPS it is because her rivers are said to have yielded more freshwater pearls than those of any other European country, that Russia has such a long and strong tradition of pearl embroidery. Before the tenth century her princes were wearing pearl sewn garments, and detailed records of her pearl fishing industry survive from a very early date. This is particularly true of the northern part of the country where the rivers in the vicinity of Novgorod were rich in pearl-bearing molluscs, and the pearls that were sewn upon the vestments and hangings of the great cathedral of St Sophia, came from the tithe levied on the industry, which was paid each year in kind into the Patriarch's chest.

So profitable did all this become that Peter the Great attempted to regularise the industry and to establish some sort of control over it, not only by drawing up a code of instructions governing the fishing itself, but also by appointing overseers responsible for its administration and for collecting the substantial revenues accruing therefrom. These were much sought after appointments and were given only to the most trustworthy officials. The biggest and most perfectly formed pearls were, of course, paid into the treasury of the Tsar himself.

It seems to have been common practice in most countries for the fisherman to place each pearl as he found it, in his mouth, retaining it there for at least two hours. Afterwards he wrapped it in a damp cloth, thrust it inside his shirt, and kept it for a long while against the warmth of his body. This was thought to harden the pearl and to give it a better colour and lustre. In grading them it was usually the smaller or *half pearls* that were set aside for embroidery. Two distinct methods of pearl sewing seem to have existed, the names of which are best translated as *Threading* and *Placing*. By *Threading*, a mesh of pearls was created quite independent of the fabric to which it was later applied; but in the second method the pearls were stitched directly to the fabric—that is, they were *Placed* upon it—often in combination with metal threads and surface stitchery of great richness and elaborate design. These were both quite complicated techniques and pearl embroidery was considered to be an art that was entirely separate from, and even more difficult than other methods of embroidery.

All the old instructions for pearl embroidery say clearly that the material must be very tightly stretched, and from their wording we see that it was wound on to the rollers in such a way that they were *on top of* and not as we would often have it today, *below* the area to be worked. This can be seen in the illustrations in, for example, Diderot and many other eighteenth-century books. The design is, as it were, rolled in upon

68 *By the nineteenth century Russian pearl embroidery had become, in common with other European needlework, overloaded and sentimental. These two angels are made in a type of raised or stumpwork but lack the vigour of the work of former centuries; a few sequins and blue beads are scattered on their robes, and pearls outline their haloes and are thickly sewn on the font   In the possession of Lady Zia Wernher*

itself, and the advantage lies in the fact that a narrow board can then be placed across the fabric and supported on the rollers, thus providing a platform on which the hand can rest while the stitches are made. In this way the most delicate fabric is protected from dirt and the design is not rubbed or smudged.

The pearls, we are told, were first scattered on a piece of black velvet or dark cloth and threaded on white silk or linen thread. This was then wound on to a small spool or bobbin called a *viteïka* which was used to pull the thread tight as sewing proceeded. In *Placing* the thread was sometimes couched, but more often sewing was rendered even more secure by making a knot between each pearl. With the left hand below the frame, the needle was passed up in front of the pearl to the right hand, and the literal translation of the instructions reads: 'When the needle arrives with the thread, she slips off the needle and makes a knot; she then re-threads the needle and returns it.' So each pearl rested in its own small depression, isolated by a knot on either side from its neighbours, thus ensuring that if the thread became chaffed and broke only one pearl

was lost, its absence would be quickly seen, and by finding a replacement that fitted exactly into the depression, a new pearl could be inserted without visably spoiling the symmetry or the colour.

If the design occupied such a position, as it frequently did, that it was out of reach of one pair of hands—say in the centre of a frontal or dossal—two women became involved in fastening the pearls, one working above and one below the frame. The pearls were threaded into a lace like mesh and spread on the framed material. The first worker, resting her hands on the board placed between the rollers, made a stitch across the thread, and passed the needle down to her companion who was crouching below. She then pierced a small hole in the fabric a short distance ahead, and through this the needle was returned to her from below. The *viteïka* was constantly used to pull the thread tight.

But the pearl sewing for which Russian women are most widely known was done on their own elaborate head-dresses. These were their most highly prized possessions and were handed down from mother to daughter through successive generations. Usually they were made upon a foundation of velvet, and literally dripped with loops and bunches of pearls. A German traveller records, perhaps not very kindly, how in 1845 he stopped at a café in a small town in southern Russia and being struck with the remarkable beauty of the proprietor's daughter who waited upon him and his friend, he began to compliment her on her appearance. He was surprised, however, to discover that she was less vain of her looks than of the truly magnificent, glittering pearl cap she wore upon her head. 'They wear these *mushkas*,' he goes on, 'every day, and even when they are clad almost in rags, their heads are often still covered with pearls. We inquired of our beautiful waitress whether she was not in perpetual dread on account of her pearl cap and how she protected it from thieves, and she answered that she wore it on her head all day and at night placed it in a casket which rested under her pillow.'

Figs 69, 70 and 73, are drawn from *Russkoe Shit'e Zhemchugom* by L. I. Yakunina.

69

71

70

69 Abraham's three angelic visitors was a favourite subject with Russian painters and embroiderers. They are shown here outlined with pearls and dated 1601
Drawn from a photograph

70 Russian ikon embroidered and hung with pearls
Residentzplatz Museum, Munich

71 Red cloth embroidered in pearls with gold cord along the edge; an example of the type of beautifully rich design used in Russian ecclesiastical embroidery, sixteenth century
Drawn from a photograph

ICXC

63

73

72

72 Byzantine embroidery with pearls
Byzantine Museum, Athens

73 The 'viteïka' used for pulling threaded pearls tight during sewing
Drawn from a photograph

ONE is apt to think that artificial pearls must be a comparatively recent invention, but indeed this is far from the truth, and for over three hundred years they have been 'sought after for the Ornament and Pleasure of Ladies'. They are cheap but they break very easily, and therefore each should be scrutinised carefully before it is stitched in place, and those that appear to be frail or badly formed rejected.

In 1680 a Parisian rosary maker named Jacquin discovered a process by which *essence d'Orient*, a preparation made by grinding the silvery scales of very small fish, could be induced to attach itself to the inner surface of the thin walls of little glass spheres. He filled the crevices that remained with white wax and a new type of bead had been invented which was to be used extensively for embroidery on dress. It was, however, by no means the first method by which artificial pearls were produced.

Eleven years earlier another Frenchman had published a book entitled *The Art of Glass* to which he appended three sections, one on mirror making, one on the manufacture of glass eyes (complete with illustrations), and a third intended to explain how pearls might be imitated 'with such exactness of Lustre as to leave it in the power of any to distinguish them easily from the True and Natural ones'.

'Tis some years' he says, 'since the Use of these was introduced into France' and he gives several different recipes for making them, collected presumably from other European countries, perhaps one might guess from Italy. *To Imitate Fine Oriental Pearl*—and it is always *pearl* as a collective noun—one must it seems 'take very fair Oriental Seed Pearl and reduce it to impalpable Powder on a Marble; dissolve afterwards in Mercury-Water, or clarified Juice of Lemons; if this be not effected quick enough, set it in a cucurbit (a gourd) over warm Ashes, and be very careful to take the Cream (which in a little time will appear at top) immediately off, so withdraw the Dissolution from the fire, and let it settle a little; this done pour it gently into another Glass Body, and keep it apart, you'll have the Pearl in a Paste at the bottom, and with it fill your gilded Plate Moulds, made to what bigness, or form, you think fit, pressing the Paste with the Silver Spatula, and so shut them up four and twenty hours; after you must take and bore them through with a Porker's Bristle, close up the Moulds, and leave them in the Oven in a Paste of Barley Dough, which being half Baked draw out and open, taking away all the Pearl, and steep them in the Dissolution just before directed to be kept apart, putting them in and out several times; so close them in their Moulds and Bake them again like Paste as before, only let this last be almost burnt up before you

65

74 *Typical mid-Victorian pearl embroidery from the panel of a wedding dress. Detail of the repeating pattern over which was suspended a deep pearl fringe*
In the possession of Miss H. Pinder

draw it out; thus you'll have the Pearl well baked and hardened. This done draw it out, open all the Moulds, take away the Pearls, and string them on one or more Gold or Silver Threads; steep them in Mercury-Water for about a Fortnight; after this dry them in the Sun in a well closed Glass Body, so you'll have very fine and splendid Pearl'.

Though recommended as being 'very like the Natural', *Counterfeit Pearl* was apparently made of greatly inferior materials, and by a far less complicated process: 'Take Chalk well purified, and separated from its grossness and sand, make Paste thereof, and so mould it up like Pearl in a Mould for that purpose; pierce these through with a Bristle, and let them afterwards dry before the Sun, or for more dispatch in an Oven, till they receive a just hardness; then string them on very fine Thread of Silver, colour them over lightly with Bole-Armoniack, diluted in Water of Whites of Eggs, and then drench them with a Pencil and Fair Water, and so apply Leaf-Silver all over, and let them dry; this done, burnish them, till they shine very finely. To give them the true Colour of Pearl, make a Glue of Parchment, or rather Vellom Shavings; . . . when you use this Glue you must warm it in a flat Vessel, and then dip the string of Pearl therein, so as not

to fill the interval Inches between each Pearl, but that every one may be done all over equally; after this let them dry.'

Fashion notes of about 1838 sometimes refer to Roman Pearls and these were made by shaping small pieces of fine grained alabaster, either with a knife or on the lathe. The pearly, inside parts of oyster and other shells were then removed from the rough, outer covering, ground to powder, and mixed with either a solution of isinglass in proof spirit, or with a very white and transparent size. The beads were impaled on slender rods cut from bamboo canes and dipped into the mixture. Pots filled with earth or sand were provided into which the rods could be thrust so that the beads were supported in the air and could not touch each other. Work was, if possible, done in a warm room so that the beads dried quickly and could be dipped again and again until a sufficiently pearl-like surface was obtained.

As early as 1669 artificial pearls were being imported by the London merchants, and it is often a problem to distinguish between *Fine Oriental Pearls, Counterfeit Pearls, Roman Pearls,* and those described by Dr Johnson as being formed by 'a distemper of the creature that produces them.'

66

(a)

(b)

75 *Illustration showing the change from (a) hand sewn to (b) machine sewn pearl embroidery on two wedding dresses dated respectively 1895 and 1924*
Bethnal Green Museum, London

Crystal and jet

BY the eleventh century the practice of counting prayers on beads had become established in the Christian church. In London these *paternostres* as they were almost universally known, were made and sold in the crowded little world of medieval lanes that twisted and seethed around St Paul's churchyard. Some were costly golden beads set with jewels or pearls; others, like the rosary carried by Mary Queen of Scots at her execution, were threaded with sweet-smelling pomander beads; some were 'beades of wode'; and Diderot under the heading *Paternostier*, shows us a number of pictures illustrating the process of making beads from bone (76). It is interesting to know, in this connection, that in 1381 the stock of a London jeweller included '5 setts of paternostres of white bone for children'.

But what is particularly relevant to the present study is the discovery that in the course of time not only the word bead itself, but also certain kinds of bead that were once used for making *paternostres*, have been gradually taken over by embroidery—notably beads made of crystal, jet and coral—all of which were once credited with possessing supernatural powers.

Jet, is black and beautiful and shining. Like crystal it is listed in the early rate books and customs records; 'beades of Christall' were valued at xls. the thousand, and 'Jeats' at

iiis.iiiid. the pound, and in 1378 'one sett of beads of geet' cost sixpence. Much of it came from northern Spain, and many of the pilgrims who for centuries flocked to the shrine of St James at Compostella, must have returned to England bringing with them as souvenirs and amulets, the little jet shells, tiny hands, and paternostres that were produced there in such quantities, and which they regarded as powerful protection against witchcraft and the Evil Eye.

As long ago as the Bronze Age, jet was worked at Whitby in Yorkshire, and the monks at Whitby Abbey used paternostres of jet; but it was not until the last century that it became associated with embroidery. About 1800, a retired naval officer, Captain Tremlett, found that he could turn jet on the lathe. He entered into partnership with two jet-workers, and together they founded the first modern jet workshop. By 1850 there were fifty workshops, and by 1873 jet was the height of fashion and the number had increased to two hundred. The industry was, of course, greatly encouraged by the fact that after the death of the Prince Consort, Queen Victoria directed that all ladies presented to her must put off their colourful, flashing rubies, diamonds, and emeralds, and adorn themselves only with funereal, sombre, black jet. 'By this time our readers will have provided themselves with

68

76 Paternostier at work making rosaries of bone. From D. Diderot, 'L'Encyclopedie raisonne des sciences, des arts et des metiers', Vol. VIII (1762)

mourning for the late lamented Prince Consort,' cried the *Englishwoman's Domestic Magazine* which only a short time previously had put out the useful information that 'for the present, winter mantles are not yet discarded, and they consist of velvet trimmed with fur, and for more elegant wear, the same material trimmed with broad lace and jet,' following it with the announcement that 'nothing is more fashionable at the moment than jet and bugle ornaments'.

It is perhaps worth reprinting the instructions given by Godey in 1858 for making a chain with bunches of cut jet, a little larger than sago seeds.

A crocheted chain, six and a half yards long, is made first and then divided into four lengths without cutting. One end is tied together and pinned to the lead cushion. The instructions continue:

Thread a needle with silk, tie a knot, and fasten into the twist about two and a half inches from the end. Thread three beads and pass the needle through the first length of twist; then thread one bead, and pass through the second length; then another and pass through the third length; then another, and pass through the outside length; turn the lengths on the reverse side. Thread three more beads, pass through the twist; then repeat until there are four rows of beads in the group, with six at each edge. Now run the needle down the thread for the space of half an inch, and repeat the same. When a yard and a quarter is done, a jet clasp may be added and the chain is complete.

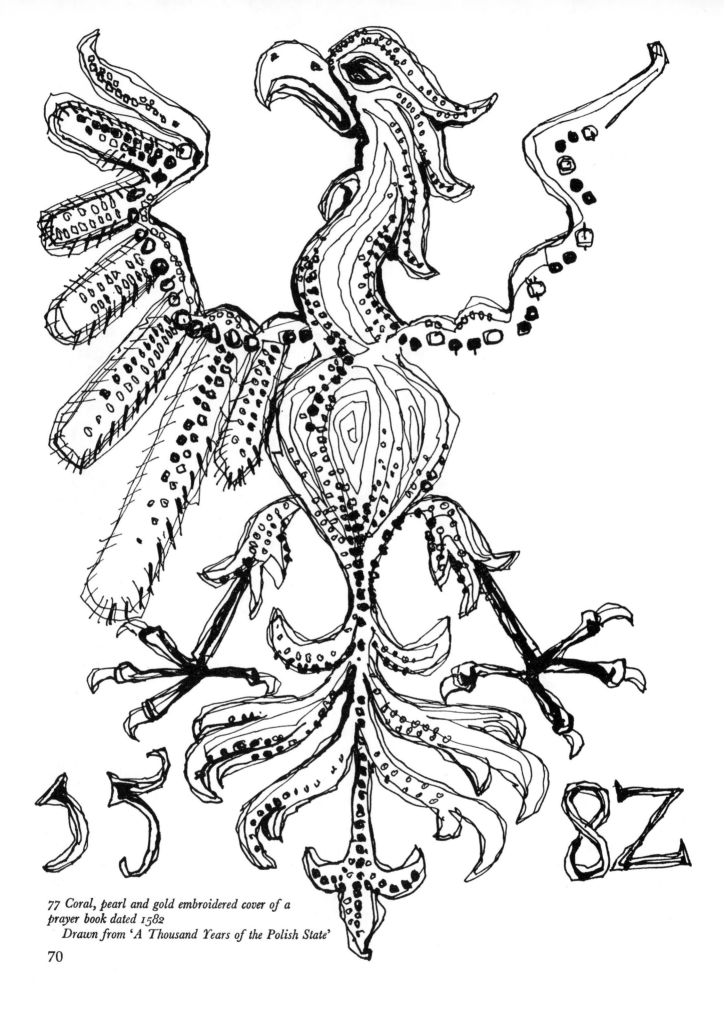

77 Coral, pearl and gold embroidered cover of a
prayer book dated 1582
   Drawn from 'A Thousand Years of the Polish State'

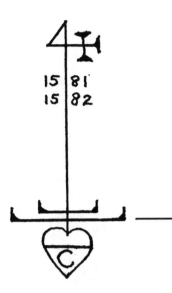

Coral embroidery

78 Trade mark of the first Coral Company

AFTER he had slain the Medusa, Perseus threw her head upon the shore, and the sea nymphs taunted it as it lay, throwing small branches of sea weed at it for the fun of watching them turn to stone. From the seeds of these twigs the ancient Greeks said that the Precious Red Coral of the Mediterranean grew. Certainly of all the substances from which beads are made, this lovely pink coral is the most mysterious, and although we think little of it today, it was once valued as highly as any gem. Ezekiel tells us that it was sold in the Syrian markets together with emeralds, broidered work, fine linen, and agates; it was prized in India as highly as pearls; it reached Tibet and China where many people considered it to be their most precious jewel; the Celtic tribes in Gaul, Britain and Ireland used it to decorate their shields, swords, and breastplates; and the Moors traded it all over North Africa. It had power over evil, and for thousands of years was used not only 'against melancholly and sadnesse, and to freshen and comfort the fainting spirits', but also as 'a pretty medicine for fevers in children, the measles, and smallpox', and for the relief of more serious diseases and disorders. Because it was costly it occurs frequently in company with pearls on medieval embroideries.

For all this, it grows very slowly and only in certain limited areas of the Mediterranean, chiefly near the islands of Sicily, Corsica, and Sardinia; off the coast of France and Catalonia; off Tunisia, Morocco, and Algiers; and in parts of the Ionian Sea. The fishermen are, of course, reluctant to disclose the location of the banks they find.

The season lasts from March to October and during that time fishing goes on night and day, ceasing only in bad weather. Fishing is carried out by means of an *engin*, a primitive piece of tackle composed of ropes and netting attached to a stout wooden cross about a yard or more in length. The larger boats carry as many as thirty *engins*. When the captain thinks he is over a bank, he lets this strange apparatus down into the sea and puts the capstan into operation. The cross is thus dragged along the rocks and stones, breaking off the coral, which is picked up in the tangles. After being landed, the coral is packed in cases and sent nowadays to Naples, Livorno, or Genoa where it is carved and polished. Until it is exposed to the air, coral is not completely hard and so the craftsmen have to work it under water.

'Beads of corrall' appear in the earliest of the customs records. Later between 1860 and 1870 they were arriving in London in very large quantities indeed, probably because a white crape bonnet with a 'voilette of white tulle, spotted with red coral beads, and trimmed with

71

79 Border pattern in small crystal beads and gold thread for an evening dress

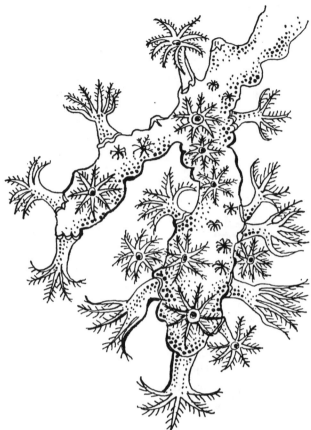

80 'Corallium nobile', the Precious Red Coral of the Mediterranean

a fringe of the same' was regarded as the height of fashion. Lady Mary Alford tells us that it was much used in Sicily and therefore the name *Sicilian* is given to all such work. Coral was also recommended a few years later, by the editor of *The Amateur's Art Designer*, for embroidery. 'This original and very beautiful kind of work,' she wrote, 'is the invention of a clever lady resident in the North of England, and I feel sure that many workers, eager for some tasteful novelty, will hail with pleasure the description I am able to give.'

The design she recommends for a book cover on a rather light blue green satin or rich silk, is illustrated in fig. 82 and to work it she gives the following instructions:

For coral embroidery a large flower, may, for instance, first be worked on the material, forming a centre with a large coral bead. Around this five or six petals must be worked in very close lines of gold thread, sewn on double, the centre of each petal being completed by a row of five steel, gold, or coral beads, the latter forming the centre. Round the flowers, scrolls of close laid gold work must be laid, and these must enclose or bear upon them coral beads, or sprays of various shapes, each one, as well as the large bead forming the centre of the flower, being edged with steel and coral beads, alternately threaded together.

81 Head of the Medusa

*82 Two designs for coral embroidery
From the 'Amateur's Art Designer' July 1890*

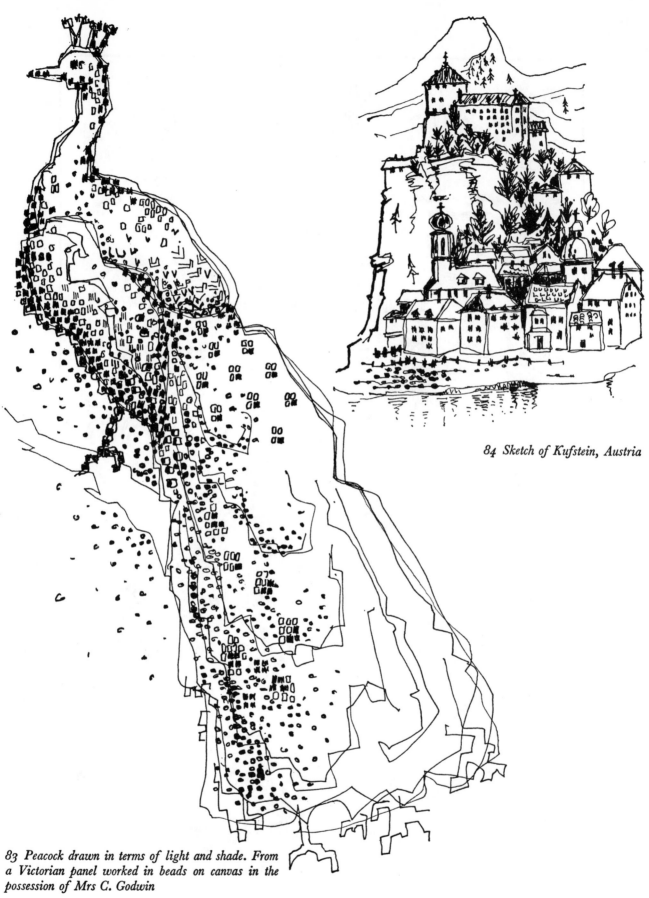

84 *Sketch of Kufstein, Austria*

83 *Peacock drawn in terms of light and shade. From a Victorian panel worked in beads on canvas in the possession of Mrs C. Godwin*

74

The manufacture of embroidery beads

GLASS is produced when sand (*silica*) and an alkali (*sodium* or *potash*) are fused together at very high temperatures. How and when it was discovered is not known. We can only assume that some man with an inquisitive mind, sifting through the refuse of a potter's kiln or a smelter's furnace, noticed the shining fragments amongst the waste, collected them together, re-heated them, and found himself with a clear liquid which hardened as it cooled into so durable a substance that neither climate nor age corrupted it, and which had what were to him two almost unearthly properties—it was transparent, and it cast practically no shadow. He made a glass rod, cut pieces from it with his tongs while it was still soft, shaped them in his fingers, and bored holes so that he could thread his new beads on a string. Alternatively he formed a series of hollows in a lump of clay, set a short stick in each, and filled them with molten glass. When this hardened he withdrew the sticks and shook out the flat disc-shaped beads. In time he found that by using sand from different localities, containing traces of copper, iron, manganese, lead or zinc, he could make coloured glass. He kept the proportions in which he mixed these elements to himself, and on his death bequeathed their secret formulae to his sons. In this way glass-making became the great hereditary craft which it remains today. Finally, when he learnt to introduce a bubble of air into molten glass, the art of glass blowing began, a process which is directly involved in the production of embroidery beads.

Glassblowers have a language all of their own. They are piece workers and their working day is called a *turn*. They call glass *metal*. The ingredients for making glass are melted in *pots*, a deceptively small word for a large hooded vessel which is made entirely by hand from coiled clay. The *footmaker* withdraws a *gathering* of molten glass from the pot on the end of his *blowing iron*; he *marvers* or rolls it backwards and forwards across a mirror smooth table called a *marver*. There is a hiss of water and a wisp of steam as the *servitor* takes it from him and shapes, blows and tools the glass before he in turn hands it to the *gaffer* who rotates the iron along the extended arms of the *chair* on which he sits, developing and completing the article with the kind of casual expertise which can only make the onlooker wonder. It is carried away by an apprentice to be annealed in the *lehr* or cooling oven, and the process, apparently quite effortless, is set in motion once again.

These three men work together as a *chair*; if they move from one firm to another they go as a *chair*, the *gaffer* being the senior craftsman of the group. So great are the skills involved that it is said to take upwards of three generations to

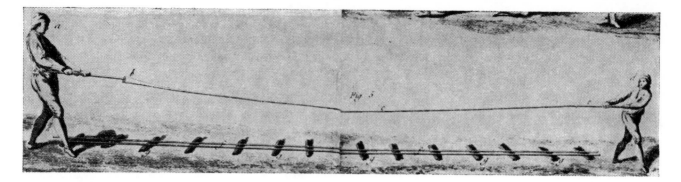

85 A master and his apprentice backing away from each other as they draw out a long thin cane or tube of glass
From D. Diderot, 'L'Encyclopedie raisonne des sciences, des arts et des metiers', Vol. x

make a *gaffer*, and most glassmakers trace their ancestry back much further than this. The tools are few and practical; the *chair* and the *marver* have probably been in use for scores of years.

The starting point in the manufacture of embroidery beads is a tube or cane of glass called *canna* in Italian, and *röhre* in German. Each is produced by slightly inflating a *gathering* on the end of a blowing iron, into which a *punty* or metal rod is introduced in such a way that the bubble closes round it. The rod is then seized by an apprentice (called in Venice a *tirador*), who runs with it down the glasshouse drawing out a long thin tube as he goes. It is laid on a row of wooden supports which have been placed on the floor at intervals ready to receive it. Alternatively, the *gatherings* on two blowing irons are united and the men walk rapidly away from each other until the glass is beginning to cool and will stretch no further. Frail rods of over one hundred feet are drawn in this way. They are cut into more manageable lengths, bundled together and pushed through a chopping machine.

Some of their roughness is removed in the next process when the beads are placed in wooden barrels filled with water and set to revolve round and round until every particle of dirt is washed away. They emerge clean, clear, and ready for colouring.

The canes are not necessarily made of colourless glass; very often colours are melted with the other ingredients in the *pot*, and when this happens, what is called *natural coloured glass* is produced, as opposed to *clear crystal glass*. In the latter instance the beads can be coloured with analine dyes or more permanently lustred with enamels. Enamelling requires both experience and judgement as each colour has to be fired at a different temperature, so beads coloured in this way are correspondingly more expensive.

Schmelzperlen is the German name for the final warming and polishing process which takes about two or three hours, and in which anything from twenty to fifty kilos of beads are handled at one time. They are fed slowly into a long tunnel-like machine, and gradually heated to six or seven hundred degrees centigrade. The heat slightly softens the exterior of the beads as they move along the conveyor belt inside the tunnel, and they become readily smoothed and polished by the abrasive action of a grinding stone with which they ultimately come in contact. In a shower of glittering coloured drops they fall again into a wooden box, and are ready to be riddled through a series of sieves and thus graded into the sizes in which they are sold.

A home industry

EMBROIDERY beads are made in Kufstein, Austria; Jablonec und Nisou, Czechoslovakia; Gmund, West Germany; and in Murano; they are often despatched from the factory loose, but to meet the requirements of some customers they have to be threaded. In Austria and Germany this has become economically unpractical, but in the Castellane district of Venice it is still a fairly common home industry, and one in which the method of working has remained almost unaltered over a very long period of time. Figure 86 is drawn from a water-colour sketch in an Italian manuscript of the eighteenth century, and apart from the dress, could easily have been made in Venice today.

Probably the beads will be kept in a large wooden box under the kitchen table from which the woman—called *infilatrici di conterie* (*conterie* being early adopted in Venice as a general term for the commoner kinds of beads)—fills her wooden scoop and sets it on her lap, with the wide end beside her left hand. She takes up a skein of glazed cotton which is slightly stiff and therefore not easily tangled. When she cuts it, threads of the required length are immediately available. She ties them around her body just below her arms, and withdraws them one at a time, to thread her needles. These are between seven and eight inches in length and are very flexible. The number used varies according to

the size of the beads but a good worker claims to be able to manipulate at least forty needles at once. When the needles are ready the threads are straightened, knotted together at one end,

86 'Infilatrici di conterie'. Drawn from an eighteenth-century manuscript, Correr Museum, Venice

and passed once or twice round the scoop to keep them out of the way. The needles are bunched together in the right hand and spread out into a fan with the left. Holding them between the thumb and first finger so that the eyes emerge at the back of the hand between the first and second fingers, she plunges the fan in and out of the beads on the scoop, causing them to pass down the needles by tapping the fan with the side of her left hand. This produces a small, busy, shuffling sound.

When the needles are full, the fan is as it were closed, and the beads are pushed down on to the threads. The fan is spread again and the shuffling sound comes back into the room. It is all very neatly and dextrously done, and as the threads fill up they are piled on the shallow end of the scoop.

Naturally, each thread does not receive the same number of beads, and eventually this has to be corrected. The unfilled space between the last bead on each thread and the eye of the needle is measured and a limited number of beads added, so that the shortest gaps are filled. These needles are then laid down; a further limited number added, and more needles laid down. This is repeated until only about half a dozen needles remain incomplete, and these are finished individually.

Until this stage is reached, the knotted end of the threads has been held securely under the tray, about twelve inches being left unbeaded. The knot is now untied and a length of beads pushed down. It is measured between two notches cut on the side of the scoop, doubled in half, and the ends tied together so that it becomes a bunch. This process is repeated until a pile of neatly tied bunches has replaced the long, loose strings of beads on the scoop. They are dropped into a basket on the floor, exactly as illustrated in the two-hundred-year-old manuscript.

Embroidery beads are called *rocailles* in the trade. They are sub-divided as follows:

Round Rocailles or *Seed Beads* which have round holes, i.e. they are round both inside and out, *Toscas* or *Square Rocailles* which have square holes, i.e. they have square holes but are round outside, and *Charlottes* which are faceted on the outside.

They are listed on the manufacturers' trade cards according to size and colour, under such headings as: Natural-silverlined, Colour-lined, Lined alabaster, Coloured chalk, Coloured alabaster, Coloured silverlined, with round or square holes—the brilliance of the colour of these beads being increased by the square holes —and Metallic.

Various names are also used to indicate the different sizes of the bunches into which *rocailles* are threaded: *Pari, Hrma, Klapat, Ameri, Introc, Kili, Victoria, Nyassa,* and *Niger.* Each string in a bunch measures fifty centimetres and is folded to twenty-five centimetres (approx. 9.84 inches), and contains about one thousand beads. A string of one thousand small beads is called a *mass.* The London merchants import their beads by the fifty kilo case.

Bead making in America

THE uniquely important place held by beads in the economy of the sixteenth and seventeenth centuries can best be illustrated by a short account of the efforts made by the first English colonists to establish a glassmaking industry in America.

The London merchants who formed themselves into a company to sponsor this first expedition were far-sighted and hard-headed. In 1606 they despatched five hundred men from the Port of London to explore the possibilities of setting up certain industries in what was known as the English Colonies. One of these specifically mentioned was glassmaking.

The leader of the expedition, Captain Christopher Newport, was able to carry home a satisfactory report on the possibility of setting up a glasshouse. Apparently all that was lacking was the skilled men and their tools.

While he was back in London the settlers probably chose the site for the glasshouse 'in the woods a myle from James Town', at a place still called Glass House Point; and when he returned with, amongst other artisans, 'eight Dutchmen and Poles', together with the necessary equipment, hopes must have run very high. When he returned once more to London at the end of the year, Captain Newport was able to take with him their first 'tryal of glasse'.

Then came the terrible period too aptly called The Starving Years, and the first glassmaking venture was over.

The idea was revived in 1621, when a certain Captain William Norton, not a glassmaker himself but a man with some money to invest and a taste for adventure, was granted a patent by the London Company to 'sett up a Glasse furnace and make all manner of Beads & Glasse'. He took out with him his family, his servants, a gang of six Italian glassmakers with their families, and a letter to the authorities in Virginia which read: 'we commend unto you Captain Wm Norton, who is now sett out by the general Company and many private Adventurers (for the) erecting of a Glasse Worke . . . and especially have a care to seat him neare some well inhabited Place, that neither his Gange be subject to Surprise, nor the Commodities of Glasse and Beads be vilified by too common Sale to the Indians.'

The Italians were temperamental, the glasshouse blew down in a storm, the Indians were in a mood for massacre, and by 1624 Captain Norton had given up completely.

Although archaeologists have dug and sifted, and have even uncovered the furnaces and the outlines of the floor of the first glasshouse, they have never found beads at Jamestown, and the credit for making the first glass beads on American soil must be passed to the Dutch and Spanish. Nevertheless, the manufacture of 'Beads & Glasse' was one of the first of the great American industries.

Beadwork of the American Indians

THE remarkable amount of bead embroidery created by the Indian women of North America during the last century was worked in two simple and uncomplicated stitches, (a) *Overlaid* or *Spot* stitch which had by far the widest distribution, being extremely adaptable and therefore used not only for covering large surfaces with a solid mass of beads, but also for the most delicate outline work; and (b) *Lazy* stitch which was, as its name implies, more rapidly worked, but suitable only for all-over patterns and borders. Many groups of beaders were, however, familiar with both methods of working.

For *Spot* stitch the beads are threaded, laid along the lines of the pattern, and held in place by making a couching stitch with a separate thread, between every two or more beads. When the material is leather the needle does not penetrate the fabric completely but rather passes through it, parallel to the surface, in such a way that no stitch is visible on the wrong side. For *Lazy* stitch, which is usually worked across a pattern, a knot is made in the thread, the needle pushed through to the right side of the leather, and the required number of beads threaded; they are then pushed closely together and the needle re-enters the leather, pulling the stitch tight. It emerges again immediately above the last stitch at the point where the next row of beads is to be laid.

The Indians had been using this form of stitchery for many centuries before the coming of the white man. About the beginning of the Christian era, the tundra dwelling people of western Siberia began to stitch the white hairs plucked from the ruff of the reindeer to the seams and hems of their clothing, thus concealing or decorating them most adequately. This simple form of embroidery spread gradually to Canada by way of the ancient cultural bridge between Asia and Alaska across the Bering Strait, and in the course of time the Indians found that they could use the quills of the porcupine for the same purpose and with even more attractive effect, and so they developed their highly personal porcupine quillwork. Both forms of decoration

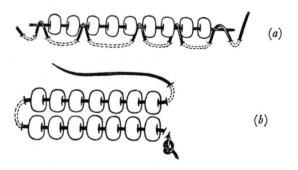

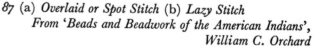

87 (a) *Overlaid or Spot Stitch* (b) *Lazy Stitch*
From 'Beads and Beadwork of the American Indians',
William C. Orchard

had much in common; the hairs and the quills were equally well coloured with vegetable dyes; and stored in bundles until needed; both had to be moistened before they could be manipulated to make them pliable and therefore the worker often held them in her mouth; and both were fastened to the skins in the same way. Quillwork did, however, develop rather more complicated geometric patterns and was in every way a more sophisticated form of embroidery.

Thus when the European beads eventually appeared, suitable patterns and a convenient method of stitchery were already in existence to greet them, and in fact a few beads were often added to hair or quillwork. Indian beadwork can therefore be aptly described as 'the child of a marriage between porcupine quillwork and commercial glass beads.' Like the Africans, the Indians were highly idiosyncratic in their choice of beads. Prior to 1900 traders' sample cards show that more than eighty colours were available, but on the whole the women showed little disposition to experiment and used only seven or eight of them.

Anthropologists who have made a special study of the subject—and the beadwork of the Amerindians is the only branch of bead embroidery which has been fully examined and recorded—warn us that contrary to popular belief, most of the patterns had no special mystical significance; and that although from time to time certain symbols and mythological creatures like the raven and the thunderbird are represented, no hidden meanings or messages can necessarily be read into them. They do, nevertheless, provide us with some interesting patterns and colour arrangements which are particularly suitable for weaving.

When, largely through the mission schools, the Indians were introduced to European floral designs, they seized upon them eagerly, and beaded scrolls and flowers were soon lavished over a hundred different objects from clothing and harness to hunters' pouches and baby cradles; even altar frontals made of leather and heavily beaded in this way made their appearance. The habit of cutting out leaf and flower shapes on paper, tacking them to the fabric, padding them with a shred of wadding, and sewing long threads full of beads over them in raised loops, was also practised.

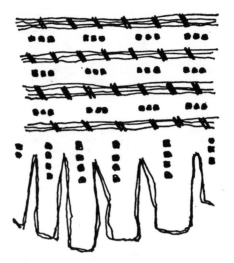

88 Reindeer hair embroidery and beadwork on a woman's apron, Siberia   *Pitt Rivers Museum, Oxford*

89 Dyed porcupine quill embroidered pattern from a fur-topped mitten, South Dakota   *Pitt Rivers Museum, Oxford*

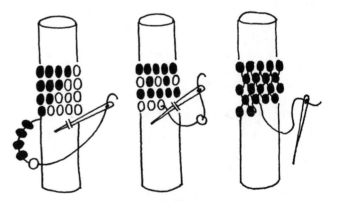

90 The Indians were familiar with several different ways of attaching beads to cylindrical surfaces, such as the handles on rattles and clubs. They were first bound with leather or fabric and then (i) enough beads to go halfway round the handle were threaded and secured with a stitch, the second half threaded, secured, and so on; (ii) beads were secured individually with a looped stitch; (iii) the handle was surrounded with a ring of beads, additional beads being drawn up in between those in the first row

81

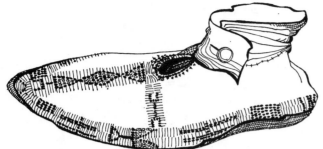

91 Moccasin using lazy stitch

92 Bead embroidered baby cradle

Pitt Rivers Museum, Oxford

(a) Detail of embroidery

92(a)

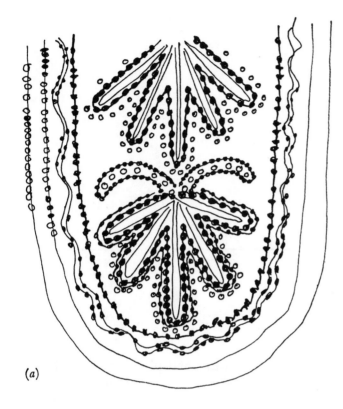

(a)

(b)

93 (a) (b) *Two beaded moccasin patterns*
Pitt Rivers Museum, Oxford

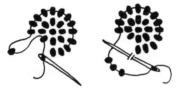

94 Two methods used by the Indians for making beaded
rosettes to ornament war bonnets, bags, and pouches

Wampum

OF all the words connected with beads and beadwork, wampum is probably the most misused. It seems to attract to itself every kind of romantic notion and misconception, and is often loosely used to describe any form of Amerindian bead embroidery.

True wampum—a word said by some to be derived from *wamp-ompe-ag* meaning 'it is made of shell', or to be the Iroquois word for a mussel—is made from the inside of the clam shell, and is a long, cylindrical bead either purple or white in colour. One of the early travellers writing in 1794 tells us that before the Europeans came to North America, the Indians used to make them strings of *wampom* chiefly of small pieces of wood of equal size, stained either black or white. Few were made of *muscles*, for not having the proper tools, they spent much time in finishing them, and yet the work had a clumsy appearance. But the Europeans soon contrived to make strings of *wampom* both neat and elegant, and in great abundance. It would, indeed, have been an arduous and difficult task to make so long a hole in so hard a shell with a stone tipped drill, and it is therefore safe to assume that most of the wampum we see today in museums was made after the introduction of iron drills by Europeans.

Another writer tells us that the shell was sometimes sent in its original rough state to England and there cut into small pieces, exactly similar in shape and size to the modern glass bugles worn by ladies. This has a double significance for us, providing not only an interesting side light on the manufacture of wampum, but also a date—1799—at which bugles existed recognisably in their present form, and as such were sufficiently well known to be used as a simile. An even earlier traveller, Robert Beverley, whose *History and Present State of Virginia* was published in 1705, makes the same comparison in discussing *Peak*, one of the names applied to wampum in some places: '*Peak*', he says, 'is of two sorts, or rather two colours, one is a dark Purple Cylinder, and the other White; they are both made in size and figure alike, and commonly much ressembling the *English Buglas*, but not so transparent nor so brittle'.

Although investigators are of the opinion that the first use of wampum was for adornment, it quickly became a useful form of currency. It was also manufactured commercially by John W. Campbell who was born in 1746 and who established a wampum factory. For many years he supplied both the Indian agents and the traders with 'Indian money'. His descendants continued to make wampum until the beginning of this century.

There is no doubt, however, that the Indians themselves made quantities of wampum, much of which was formed into their celebrated wampum belts. These were more often than not intended for use in some particular ceremony, and having served their purpose, were dismantled and the beads subsequently used again. For this reason only the most important belts were preserved. They were also used as official records of treaties and land transactions; as a summons to war; and as a symbol of steadfastness in respect of the pledged word; and Europeans learnt that an Indian council could not be regarded as seriously concerned about the subject being debated unless the wampum belts were brought out. No treaty was ratified without the exchange of belts.

The belts were woven by women on long strands of leather or vegetable fibre, both ends of the warp being passed through the holes in a piece of skin to keep them evenly spaced, and then fastened to the bow loom. The beads were worked in and out of the warp with a needle, the completed belt usually had fringed ends and consisted of anything up to two thousand beads.

The oldest wampum belt known is thought to have been made in the mid-sixteenth century. It is called the Hiawatha Belt and is in the State Museum of Albany, New York. It is reputed to have been the official record of the five nations who combined to form the League of the Iroquois, and was in charge of a hereditary keeper. It is made up of a pattern of four hollow squares outlined in white, together with a heart shaped motif in the centre. The squares and the heart are connected about mid-way by white lines. They are said to be emblems of the great peace that united the five nations, and when reversed the heart is said to assume the appearance of a tree—the Great Tree of Light—under which the five nations sit in council.

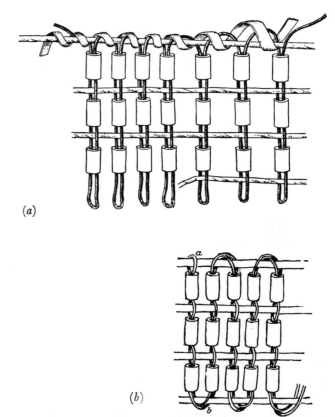

(a)

(b)

95 *Technique of weaving wampum belts*
From 'Beads and Beadwork of the American Indians',
William C. Orchard

(a) *single thread weave*
(b) *double thread weave*

Zulu talking beads

TO the Zulus of Natal who first received beads from the Portuguese and later from both the Dutch and English, probably belongs the claim to have discovered one of the most original ways of using them. Threaded on fibre made from the inner bark of the fig tree, they treat them as a means of communicating their thoughts from one to another without any verbal exchanges whatever. The substance of the message does not depend on the patterns in which the beads are arranged, but on the colours themselves, and on the relative amounts of each colour involved. White, for example, is the colour of love, and to show the depth of her affection for him and how it permeated through every part of her life, a girl would send her lover a piece of beadwork in which white beads were arranged between the other colours and predominated numerically over them all.

Like all other races and tribes, the traders found that only certain established colours were acceptable to the Zulus, and to these they gave special names. For blue beads they used the native word for a dove; for dark blue the name for the ibis; for yellow which denoted wealth, the word for the young Kaffir corn; for green beads there was the young green grass; pink expressed poverty; large beads of any colour were *amapohlo*, or eggs; and striped beads were called after the striped grasshoppers that often infested their crops.

The messages themselves were called *incwadi* or *ubala abuyise* which means literally 'one writes

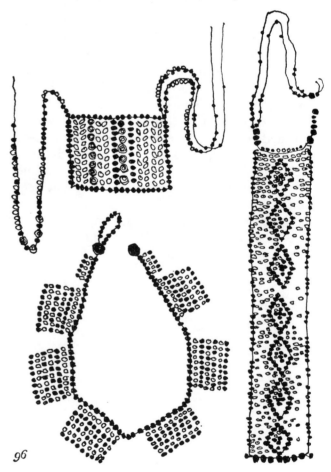

96

in order that the other should reply', and so they have come to be called letters or talking beads. In this way a Zulu girl will present her lover with a 'letter' and expect his visit in return. Perhaps it will be the simplest form of letter, just a single bead string in two colours—white and pink. The meaning would be that she realises that the man is poor (pink), and she asks him to work hard to get cattle for the bride price necessary to purchase her from her father or guardian, as she is very much in love (white) with him.

A variety of different bead ornaments are used in this way and a Zulu man is proud of his letters and hangs them all round his neck to show how much he is loved by one, or by a number of girls.

In reading a letter the string which passes round the neck is read first, commencing at the fastening, and on the whole the string is the most important part of the letter. In the case of a square or an oblong the message is read from the edge inwards, but the actual border pattern is for the sake of ornament only and has no special meaning.

The letters are woven between the fingers or on a simple loom. Lines of white, red, green, blue and black beads, threaded together could be interpreted in some such fashion as this: My heart is pure and *white* in the long weary days. My eyes are sore and *red* by looking for you so long. I have become *green* and sickly. If I were a dove—*blue*—I would fly to your home and pick up food at your door. Darkness—*black* —prevents my coming to you. But my heart is pure and white . . . and the whole message is repeated several times, until the beadwork is large enough to be an adequate and acceptable offering.

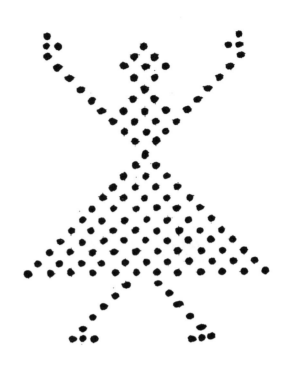

97 *Figure from plaque on a Zulu beadwork necklace*

98 *Zulu beaded dolls*

Peasant bead embroidery

IT is hard to realise how many crafts were once carried out in the shelter of the great forests of Central Europe. They were small, family affairs; unpretentious and very old; the workers needed few and simple tools, and they made use of such raw materials as the neighbourhood provided. The glassmaker, for instance, required quartz sand—which he found liberally provided in such places as Bohemia—water and wood. With the latter he not only fired his furnace but also burnt it to obtain the potash without which he could not produce glass. If he lived near the coast, he burnt seaweed instead and thus acquired sodium as an alternative to potash. When times were hard or laws and overlords oppressive or unjust, he packed up his tools and moved away to another part of the forest, sometimes to another country. In this way many French Protestants, or Walloons, arrived in England during the sixteenth century from Lorraine, which was at that time, the most important glassmaking part of France. They settled in the Hampshire woodlands, in the Forest of Dean, and in Herefordshire, and when subsequently they were forbidden to burn wood, they uprooted themselves again and moved into the areas adjacent to the coalfields. Most of the places in which they worked have been cleared long ago, but occasionally they are remembered in ancient boundaries or ordnance surveys by such names as *glasshouse field* or *ovenhusfeld*.

So whether obtained from a member of her family, or bought at a fair or from a peddler, beads were usually available to a countrywoman, and sometimes she combined them with great success with the bright, coarse stitchery with which she embroidered her own and her husband's clothing.

Completely formal, repeating patterns worked entirely in beads, were popular during the last century in Bavaria and the Tyrol. They made cheerful decorations on coarse linen or flannel, and as far as can be seen, the more garish the colours the more popular they were.

Elaborate head-dresses were often made by peasant women of beads or pearls. They were worn either over or surrounding the great circlet of hair that was considered to be a woman's greatest glory.

The peasant girl (99), her face modestly veiled in a cascade of lace, and her bodice decorated with all manner of little medals, coins, discs, and chains, wears an enveloping apron over her skirt and petticoats which has been embroidered round the waist with a charming beaded pattern of flowers and leaves. It is typical of those worked in the last century.

99

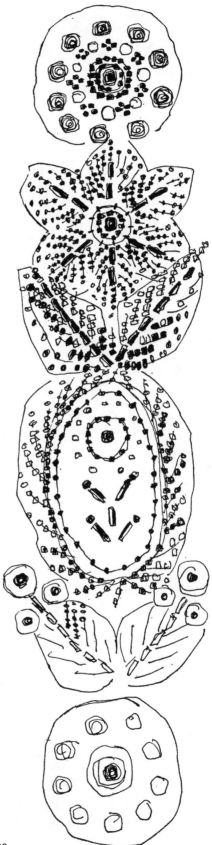

99 *Tyrolean peasant costume*
                    Bavarian State Museum, Munich

100 *Detail of beaded pattern worked round the top of the apron*

100

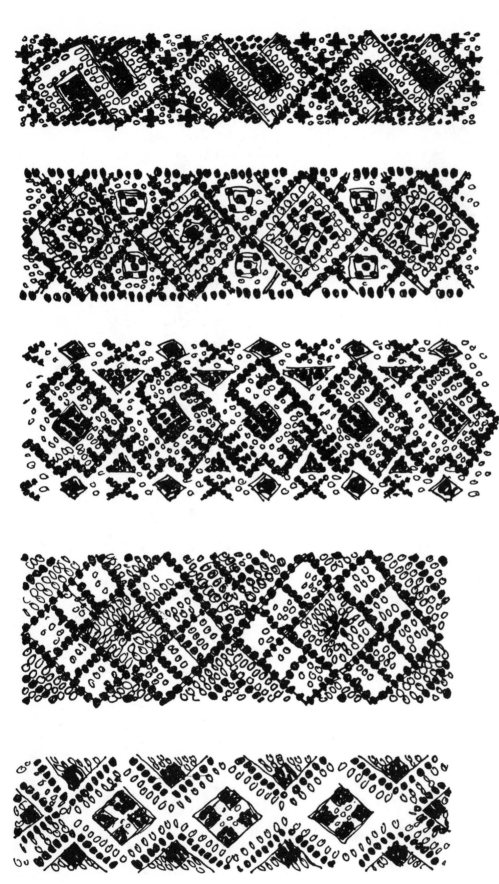

90

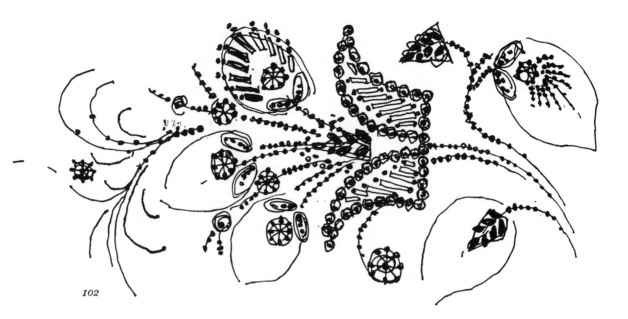

102

103

102 *Pattern on traditional Breton cap from Quimper, worked in crystal beads and bugles on black velvet, nineteenth century*
Horniman Museum, London

103-4 *Central European patterns in beads and surface stitchery from a blouse*
Gawthorpe Foundation, Burnley, Lancs.

101 Opposite: *Beaded border patterns of central Europe*

105 *Sequins and gold threads. Pattern from the crown of an embroidered cap*
From Jannina, Monastiraki Museum, Athens

106 Russian beaded motif　　　*Drawn from a photograph*

107 Russian beaded pattern

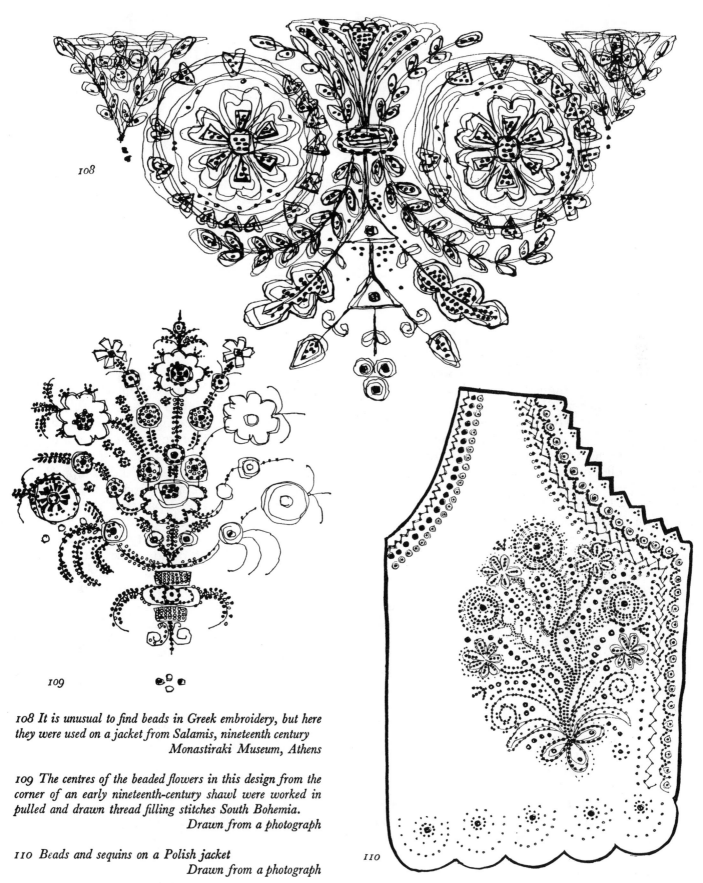

108 It is unusual to find beads in Greek embroidery, but here they were used on a jacket from Salamis, nineteenth century
Monastiraki Museum, Athens

109 The centres of the beaded flowers in this design from the corner of an early nineteenth-century shawl were worked in pulled and drawn thread filling stitches South Bohemia.
Drawn from a photograph

110 Beads and sequins on a Polish jacket
Drawn from a photograph

93

Part II Commercial Beading

Beading by machine

ALTHOUGH machines for working simple embroidery stitches were made as early as 1828, it was not until 1891 that the first machine capable of attaching beads to a fabric was invented. By 1898 Monsieur Schweizer, the head of one of the great Parisian embroidery houses, in collaboration with a mechanical engineer named Langret—who was also his brother-in-law—had built eleven machines. Three of them he retained in his own workrooms; two were set up in each of the Iklé factories at Paris, Saint-Gall, and Plauen; and two went to the Kreimler factory at Argentéuil. Iklé tells us that '*on confectionnait de très jolis articles avec ses appareils*', but nevertheless they were not altogether an unmixed blessing. For one thing it was almost impossible to find beads that were sufficiently regular in shape and size to feed into them, and the holes were often too small to allow the needles to pass freely in and out. The beads made in Bohemia were said to be useless, and although the manufacturers at Gablonz tried to sort the beads, they found this so long and arduous a process that it became, even in those underpaid days, economically impossible, and they quickly dropped it. Metal beads, on the contrary, were desirable in every way, but produced articles so heavy that the already over-clothed ladies of fashion declined to wear them.

For three years Iklé and his associates tried to overcome these difficulties, but in the end the project had to be abandoned in favour of a method that had been developed at Luxeuil on the Cornely machine. Here the problems had been solved by stringing the beads and then winding the thread on to bobbins, and although additional complications arose especially when the thread, as it frequently did, snapped, the results were considered reasonably satisfactory. Besides, the long linear patterns already in use for machine embroidery could, it was found, be worked with equal facility in beads. The endlessly revolving braid work patterns were particularly suitable, and so one finds the familiar *vermicelli* pattern being worked not in braid but in beads.

111

94

112

111–13 Bead embroidery drawn from 'La broderie mécanique',
1829–1930 by E. Iklé

113

95

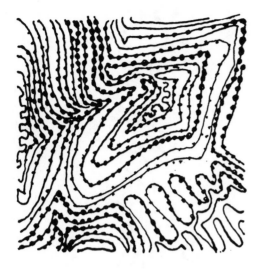

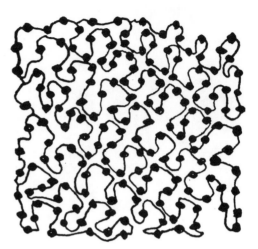

114 Vermicelli and other linear patterns

116–17 Examples showing clear glass beads and black beads threaded alternately and stitched by machine to net

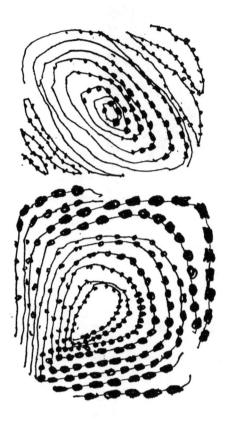
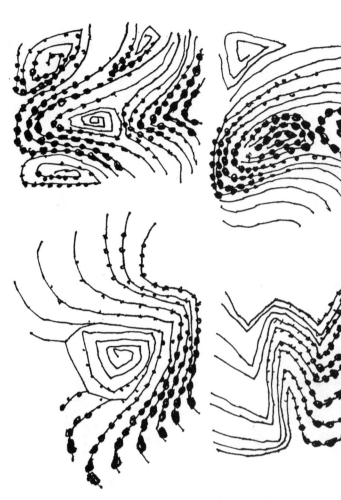

115 Patterns evolved from knots in wood

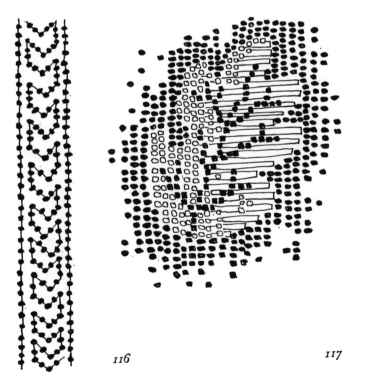
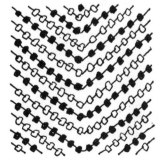

116

117

97

118-26 Drawings taken from the book of traveller's samples

119

The illustrations 118 to 126 are all taken from a book of traveller's samples which was put together in Paris just prior to 1900. It is a cumbersome affair, measuring twenty inches by thirteen, and is six inches thick. It weighs twenty pounds. Such books and the patterns they contained were very closely guarded secrets. Salesmen were apt to carry about with them a few sheets of thin paper and a heel ball, and if they were left alone for an instant with a rival firm's sample book, the tissue paper was spread quickly over the latest patterns, rubbed with the heel ball, and carried back to the workroom to be copied. For many years this was a common form of piracy.

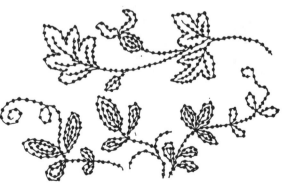

120

121

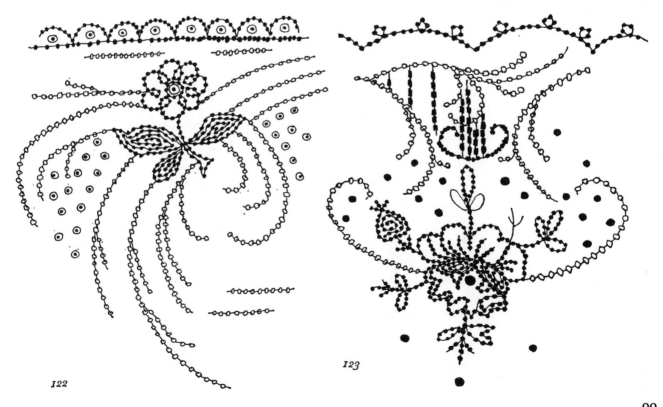

122

123

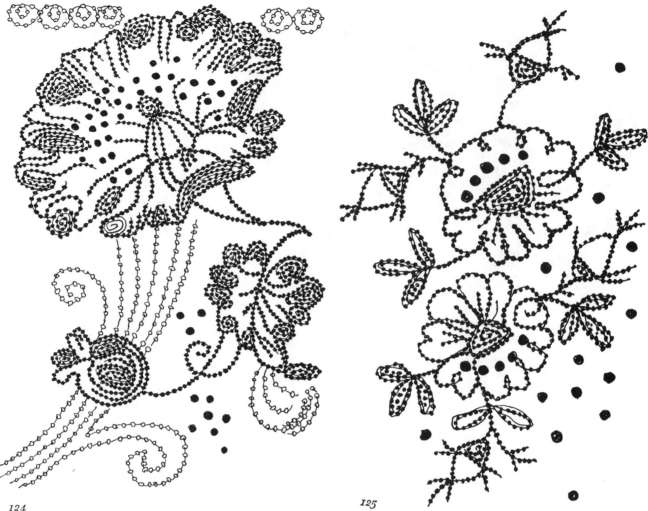

124

125

126

Tambour beading

TAMBOURING is the name used for a method of embroidering a fabric, not with needle and thread, but by means of a small, sharp hook called in French *aiguille à chaînette* or *crochet*; a word which perhaps led Thérèse de Dillmont to comment that tambouring is merely a form of crochet. The material is stretched on a round frame (*un tambour* or drum), and while the right hand operates the hook above the material, the left—which is held below the frame—presents the thread to the hook as it is driven in and out. It is impossible to guess at the age of this technique which originated many centuries ago in the Orient, from whence it spread gradually to the Levantine countries; it did not, however, reach Europe until the mid-eighteenth century when it made its appearance in Saxony and the Swiss cantons.

Exactly when and where somebody first realised that beads could be attached to a fabric by means of the tambour hook, we shall probably never know, but we will not be far wrong in thinking that the technique was first practised in the north-eastern corner of France, possibly in the vicinity of Luxeuil where, as we have seen, they had succeeded in sewing beads on the Cornely machine.

Bearing this in mind, it is interesting to discover that when this new method of tambour beading was introduced into the London work-rooms towards the close of the last century, it was called *Lunéville work*, and the map shows us that Lunéville, in the Department of Meurthe-et-Moselle, is only about eighty kilometres as the crow flies from Luxeuil. The place was famous for its cotton spinning, toys, gloves, and embroidery, and for centuries its convent was celebrated for its needlework. From inquiries in Lunéville itself, I find that bead embroidery was first introduced into the workrooms there as early as 1867, and that by 1878 a certain Louis Ferry had begun to replace the ordinary sewing needles used in his workroom by the tambour hook, the new method being known as *broderie perlée de Lunéville*.

I am convinced that unless one is able to see at first hand the beading produced in the work-rooms that supply the great couturier houses, it is utterly impossible to imagine how lovely bead embroidery can be. Like bead making and bead importing, it is a small, intense, personal occupation. The work is very costly and involves such beads, jewels, and sequins as never, in the normal course of events, find their way into the retail shops. Even the hooks are difficult to buy. They come, I understand, from one small, dark shop in a back street in Paris; its hours are irregular, and hooks are not always available even when it does happen to be open; so to each tambour beader her one hook is extremely valuable. She

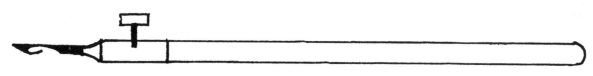

127 *Tambour beader's hook*

sits with three or four companions round a long frame on which the parts of the dress which is being embroidered are stretched. The shape of the particular sleeve, bodice, cuff or collar is outlined in tacking stitches before it comes from the manufacturer or couturier, the darts indicated, and so on; but it is not made up until after beading is finished. Joining the thread on which the beads have been purchased to one that matches the frock (usually No. 60 cotton) with a weaver's knot, she passes the beads from one to the other, winds them on a spool which is then slipped over a post on the frame, and taking the end of the cotton *below* the material, she catches it in the hook, pulls it through to the surface, secures it, and proceeds to catch up the thread between each bead as it is passed up by her left hand. In this way a series of chain stitches are made along the outline of the pattern.

To begin with, a girl will work on net or semi-transparent material, but gradually her fingers become so assured that she can tambour on velvets, satins, taffetas and so on through which she sees neither the beads nor the movements of her left hand.

When the only purpose of tambouring was to fill in a motif with chain stitches, the pattern was of course, traced on to the right side of the material and framed in the usual way; but with tambour beading the position is reversed, and

the design has to be transferred to the *wrong* side of the material, that is, to the side facing the worker, but away from the beads. To work out this highly original but simple process was perhaps the greatest achievement of Monsieur Ferry and his colleagues.

Each workroom has its own designer and assistant and their patterns are worked, in the first place, by the sample hand. A new collection is made each season and shown to the buyers and their customers. When an order is received the design is adapted to the particular garment; pricked with a power driven needle controlled by a steady, well-trained hand; and transferred to the fabric by the tracer. Beads may have to be dyed specially and this is also done in the workroom.

The more complicated, encrusted patterns cannot be worked with the tambour hook alone: a certain amount of embroidery may be done first on the Irish machine, afterwards some tambouring, and finally some hand sewing. Many of the most luxurious designs have to be sewn throughout by hand, when sequins are piled upon sequins, overlaid and overlapped, and beads and jewels combined to produce a richly ornate, gloriously colourful effect. To keep the back of the work neat, each repeat in such a pattern is completed before the next is begun.

The beaders

BUT the beaders did not always work in light, pleasant surroundings, and behind the sparkling late Victorian and Edwardian dresses is a deplorable story of 'man's inhumanity to man'—and to woman—and we must now consider the unhappy lot not only of the beaders but also of the makers of passementerie.

On 1 September 1890, *The Ladies' Magazine* published one of its usual charming pieces of feminine frippery, as nicely calculated to catch the eye of the ladies by whom it would be read as any article by a fashion journalist today. 'The autumn toilettes', we are told, 'are enriched with beautiful fringes of beads, which gracefully accentuate every movement of the wearer . . . when the fringes are of glass or jet beads, the effect is dazzling.' A contemporary illustration (128) shows just how delectable the effect might indeed have been. But the background against which these graceful movements were performed was one of abuse, aching poverty, and the misery from which there is neither respite nor release. Beading was, at that time, one of the sweated industries, with all the horrible associations that the phrase conjures up.

The practice of sweating is a very old one, and oppressed thousands of women in such trades as tailoring, millinery, dressmaking, military embroidery, buttonholing, and beading. It was the era of *The Song of the Shirt* and *The Little Match Girl*. 'We had no food,' was the defence offered by one woman who had pawned the material given out to her by her employer; and because she was unable to redeem it, she went from her squalid room, which probably served her whole family as both living, sleeping, and workroom, to prison. Her story underlines the great gulf that was fixed between those who played and laughed in the sun, and the underworld that groaned and toiled and sweated; a world inhabited by pathetic, bewildered men and women, on whom the burden of overwork rested from childhood to old age.

Government contracts for such work as embroidery on military uniforms were known to be negotiated so that a reasonable wage could be paid, and so the sub-contractor—who was most frequently the sweater—would not dare to underpay for this work, but in giving it out he would often stipulate that the woman must execute other commissions for him at sums considerably lower than those she ordinarily obtained. Many people were frightened to disclose to such inspectors as there were, the true state under which they worked, and so it was extremely difficult to collect reliable information on which parliamentary reforms could be based. However, to bring the problem to the attention of the public, the Women's Industrial Council organised an exhibition of work made under

128 'Manteaux d'hiver pour jeunes femmes et jeunes filles'
From 'Le moniteur de la mode'

sweated conditions, which was known as the *Daily News* Sweated Industries Exhibition, and was held in London in May 1906.

This idea originated in Berlin in 1904, and in the same year, the vicar of St James the Less, Bethnal Green, in the East End of London, arranged an exhibition in his church hall showing the effects of sweated labour in his parish. In spite of the fact that it lasted for only two days it attracted a great deal of attention, and paved the way for the larger and more compelling *Daily News* exhibition.

In the catalogue, Mrs Ramsay MacDonald who was particularly interested in the beaders, wrote:

A great variety of beading is done in the homes; beading jackets and mantles, trimmings and braids of various kinds, bead ornaments, beaded belts, beading of shoes, embroidery with beads and sequins, etc. The trade is as variable in rates of pay as in kinds of work, and is affected to some extent by the season, but still more by the fashion. There are sometimes periods of several years during which bead trimmings are hardly used, whilst at the present time there is a large demand for all kinds of varieties. The work is often trying to the eyes, as beads are of different sizes, shapes and colours and have to be sorted out, counted, and arranged in patterns. The examples shown in the exhibition include some done in London, and also some done in country cottages. There are villages where a woman will fetch work from London and then let it out to the villagers around, each of whom does it for a price less that paid to the middlewoman, and the sub-contracting leads to very low wages.

Women were paid $4\frac{1}{2}d$. per yard for making a bonnet fringe, and it took four hours to make a yard. It took half an hour to bead one shoe for which the pay varied between $7d$. and $9d$. a dozen pairs. Nobody, working even twelve or fourteen hours a day could hope to earn more than six or seven shillings a week.

The purchaser knew nothing about the real conditions and would certainly not have been encouraged to inquire.

The evils were so widespread both on the continent and in Britain that they even crossed the sea to America and to Australia and New

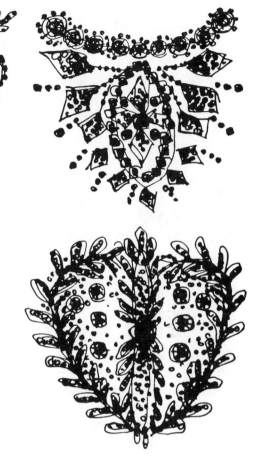

129 *Four Victorian shoe buckles*

Zealand. Underneath the surface of progress, prosperity and equality in these countries, sweating dens appeared, and spread like weeds in a new and favourable soil. In America they existed almost exclusively among the immigrants who swarmed over to what they believed to be the Land of the Free, but which in fact trapped them in a system that was every bit as vicious as that from which they thought to escape; and again the way of the reformer was hard. An attempt was made in Chicago to provide for the inspection of houses where garments were made which forebade any except members of the family to work in such dwellings. The immediate result was a large apparent increase in the size of the families of workers, as all profitable workers were straight away adopted as relatives. Finally, however, legislation in every country was gradually formulated, and the evil practices diminished and eventually vanished.

But bead embroidery occupied not only the dreary working hours of women in slums and factories, and the pretty idle fingers of the rich, but also of those unfortunate women who were thrown upon the hard world of necessity, usually through events quite beyond their control—the ladies in reduced circumstances, the genteel poor, the distressed gentlefolk.

One of the ways in which they might hope to earn a little money was by embroidery or beading.

'A deft use of the needle is a particularly ladylike accomplishment, but plain sewing is hard and wearing work,' wrote Mrs Ella Church in her book entitled *Money-Making for Ladies* that was published in New York in 1882. 'In all large cities there are emporiums, generally known as Ladies' Depositories, where ladies (for whose benefit they are intended) can deposit articles of needlework made by them for sale, receiving the proceeds when sold, after the deduction of the usual ten per cent commission; while ladies who want work done, deposit it there to be given out to the proper persons.' After numerous other worthy platitudes she ends lamely enough, 'Indian bead work has its attractions when bought of Indians and some ladies manufacture it on a very elaborate scale for fancy fairs. But what would a city shopkeeper do with it?' The prospect for the ladies, impoverished and proud, echoed hollowly. Eventually both they and the beaders must have come to detest the sparkling balls of glass and jet which they sorted, stitched, and twisted for the delight and adornment of other women's good fortune.

Passementerie

Passement, or *passemayne*, was the name by which trimming made of gold or silver braid or ribbon was originally known. The technique is a very, very ancient one and reached Europe from the Orient, where, by the Middle Ages, it had developed into an important industry. Much of it was made in Italy, but by the sixteenth century the Parisian *passementiers* were sufficiently numerous to be able to incorporate themselves into a guild, their charter being granted by Henri II in 1559. They took two crossed needles and four metal buttons as their coat of arms, St Louis as their patron saint, and the church of Les Grands-Augustins as their guild church.

The *passementiers* were divided into a number of specialist groups according to the various kinds of trimming they made; and these decorations which were used in general for four different purposes—on dress, on furniture, on military uniforms, and on the upholstery of coaches and carriages—were known as *passementerie*. By the eighteenth century French *passementerie* had reached its highest perfection, and Diderot provides us with page after page illustrating both the looms and the complicated techniques involved in making it.

To the Victorians, however, *passementerie* meant the heavy, rich ornaments, encrusted with beads, that they made by intertwining braid or cords, and with which they festooned their shapely dresses.

They were made commercially under the same sweated conditions that oppressed the beaders. These were all too vividly described in a report published in 1897 on the *passementiers* in Vienna, who, even after an apprenticeship of three years were exploited, under-paid, under-nourished, and completely at the mercy of the middle man or woman, and of the seasonal demands of the couturier houses. In a good year there was never more than nine months work, so in the other three debts piled up that could only grow larger and larger and never be effectively met. Sometimes deductions were made from her already meagre wages if the worker was one minute late; she had nowhere to wash; inadequate lighting; unendurable cold in winter, and in summer no escape from the suffocating heat that beat down on the tall old Viennese houses.

The women had black coffee and a roll or a piece of black bread before going to work, and another slice of bread at ten o'clock; for dinner at midday they took a little soup, vegetables, and bread at the nearest cheap eating house; more bread and coffee in the afternoon, and occasionally a pair of sausages made from horseflesh for supper. Too often there was no money to buy any food for this meal. The Report states that on Sundays many had either boiled horseflesh

130 *Eighteenth-century pattern for galon*
From D. Diderot, 'L'Encyclopedie raisonne des sciences, des
arts et des metiers' Vol. VIII, *1762*

or beef, but as their stomachs were unaccustomed to such food, indigestion often resulted, and they are not able to work on Monday. When they did not work, nobody paid them and there was nothing to eat.

If they were going to make their own *passementerie* ornaments Weldon's *Practical Needlework* advised their readers 'to choose a cord that was firm and wiry and readily bent into shape, and then to draw the design carefully upon a piece of stout paper, twisting the cord into the desired form by laying it frequently down upon the pattern, and keeping the strands thus shaped in place by stitches taken through the middle of the cord'. Care is needed to keep the strands of cord perfectly flat, but the knack required will soon be gained after a little practice, and the worker will be able to arrange these end foundations without the trouble of sketching a paper pattern. If two or more foundations are required, it is advisable to prepare both at once.

Having arranged the cord the work com-

mences at the centre of the ornament. It usually requires three beads to cover the cord and these are threaded, pushed down against the cord, and laid across it in a slanting direction. They are held in place with the thumb of the left hand, and the needle is passed through the strands of cord, and emerges immediately above the first beads. Three more beads are then threaded, laid side by side above the first row, held down with the left thumb, and the needle once again passed through the cord. Scarcely any stitches should be visible on the wrong side, and beading continues until the upper side of the cord is completely covered.

Large beads are sewn on to flat circles made by coiling the cord at the appropriate places on the design.

Drops, fringes, and tassels are an essential part of any *passementerie* ornament, and two or more ornaments are often looped together by festoons of beads of various shapes and sizes.

131 *Passementerie ornament with tassels*

132 *Cord laid on pattern ready for beading*

131

Part III

Dating Victorian beadwork

IT is a matter of considerable interest to many people to discover the date at which embroideries in their possession were worked, but with beadwork one is on very uncertain ground.

As a rough guide, however, I have compiled a list from magazines published during the twenty years between 1846 and 1866, in both England and America, when new patterns for beads were constantly being devised. It provides no more than the lightest possible framework from which to set out in search of more conclusive evidence in the tractless wilderness of undated beadwork that lies around us.

1846   Beaded bags with 'star bottoms'.
Beaded bags with steel and gold beads.
Crocheted purses with 'square bottoms and a fringe of gold beads'.

1848   Steel beads.

1849   Purse with gold beads and gold tassels.

1850   Knitted flowers, occasionally with beads.

1852   Hand screens with beads.

1854   Bead and bugle work.

1855   Scripture mottos.
Perforated cards worked in silk or beads.
Vine leaf patterns.

1856   Beaded bell ropes.
Hanging flower vases in beads.
Pound beads recommended.
Turkish purse made of beads in two sizes.
Mourning collar and cuffs in 'crape with seed beads and small bugles'.
Ornamental flowerpot in beads and Berlin work.

1857   Sofa cushion embroidered in beads and wool work with arabesque pattern.
Pin-cushion in which beads, not pins, make the decoration.
Candlesticks ornamented with beads.

1858   Mats with floral patterns in crystal and coloured beads.
Chair-backs and seats in beads and wool.

1859   Beaded watch cases.
Crocheted mats called 'jewelled d'oyleys' with currants, strawberries, etc. in beads.
Lappets for the hair in beads, bugles, and pearl beads.

1860   'Bugle velvet ribbon' apparently purchased ready beaded.
Flower patterns.

1861   Velvet embroidered with jet.

1862   Beaded slippers.
Needlebook in beads and Berlin work.
Beaded toilet cushions.
'Bugle trimming and crape bows with bugles for mourning.'
Raised beadwork.

1863   Fleur-de-lis banner screen with beads.

1864   Bugle passementerie.
Large beaded necklaces.
Black lace with jet on bonnets.
White crape bonnet with coral beads.
Oriental patterns for slippers with steel beads.
Bugle passementerie on silk aprons.

133 Crystal beads on canvas with background of red Berlin wool   In the possession of the author

1865   Beaded flowers. Beads left rather loosely, or sewn over glazed lining paper or calico.

1866   Beaded fringes and tassels.
Beaded photograph frames.
Belts trimmed with beads and 'seed bugles'.
Spangles and sequins.
Seed pearls and pearl beads on dress, often fringed.

Grecian patterns worked in beads.
Black passementerie 'studded with very small white beads'.
Black lace studded with jet.
Jet and bugle ornaments.
Much beadwork on wire.
Bead rosettes on bonnets.
Purse in tatting with beads.
Parasols embroidered with beads.

Part IV Pattern making

Planning a design

THERE is nothing in the records of history which leads us to suppose that women have ever invented the designs they embroider. On the contrary it is quite clear that their demands for patterns have been met throughout the centuries by professional designers and draftsmen of greater or lesser skills.

The Tudors called their designers 'drawers' and as such they flit in and out of the account books of the great households, while the Stuart ladies depended on pattern books and on the haberdashers who supplied them with 'all Sorts of Patterns for Needle Work'; and who, along with their usual stock-in-trade of embroidery materials, needles, pins, thimbles and threads, were prepared to 'Draw ye Neatest and Genteelest Patterns for Stitchery, French Quilting, Imbroidery, Crosstich, Tentstich, Point and Flourishing', or to sell 'Seats for Chairs, Screens and Carpits already drawn'.

By the end of the eighteenth century the first women's magazines, dedicated to the publication of 'whatever might tend to please the Fancy, interest the Mind, or exalt the Character of the British Fair', were encouraging their readers to become proficient in 'the wonderful art of needlework', and were printing patterns to assist them towards this praiseworthy goal, and by the time that Victoria was on the throne this trickle had become a tidal wave. The craze for 'art needlework' and beadwork was on and the most extravagant claims were made for both the patterns and the pattern makers, as is shown in this announcement which appeared in the *Englishwoman's Domestic Magazine*: '. . . a Wreath or Bouquet in Bead work for a Music Stool, in producing which no trouble or expense has been spared. . . . for the first German and French artists have, for months, been busily engaged on working out the thousand and one minute details necessary to the completion of the pattern. The model from which the pattern is taken is elegant in the extreme, the mixture of beads and wool forming a charming *tout ensemble*.'

Today, a designer or an examination candidate, faced with the problem of making a pattern for any method of embroidery, must first produce a series of what are called *roughs*. There may be six or more of these little sketches or notes, one of which will eventually be enlarged and developed with the aid of museum studies, outdoor sketches and literary material. The object in collecting this information is to stimulate the imagination, and the following illustrations show the type of research that should be undertaken when preparing a non-geometric design for bead embroidery, the subject of which is *flying swallows*. They include museum studies and notes made from photographs; sketches of grasses, flowers and reeds that are found in and around the pools frequented by swallows; as well as drawings of moths and other insects.

In all this material there are innumerable small motifs, and with their help more detailed roughs are made and experiments with light and shade, textures and colours, carried out. The

simplicity of the first roughs must be maintained and the balance between the background shapes preserved. These points can be tested by turning the design upside-down, or by looking at it in reverse in a mirror. If it is covered with a piece of tracing paper, the confusing mass of scribbled lines disappears and the strong, important ones can be examined and reconsidered if necessary.

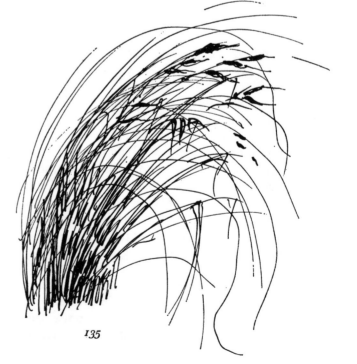

134–40 Sketchbook studies for beaded panel

135

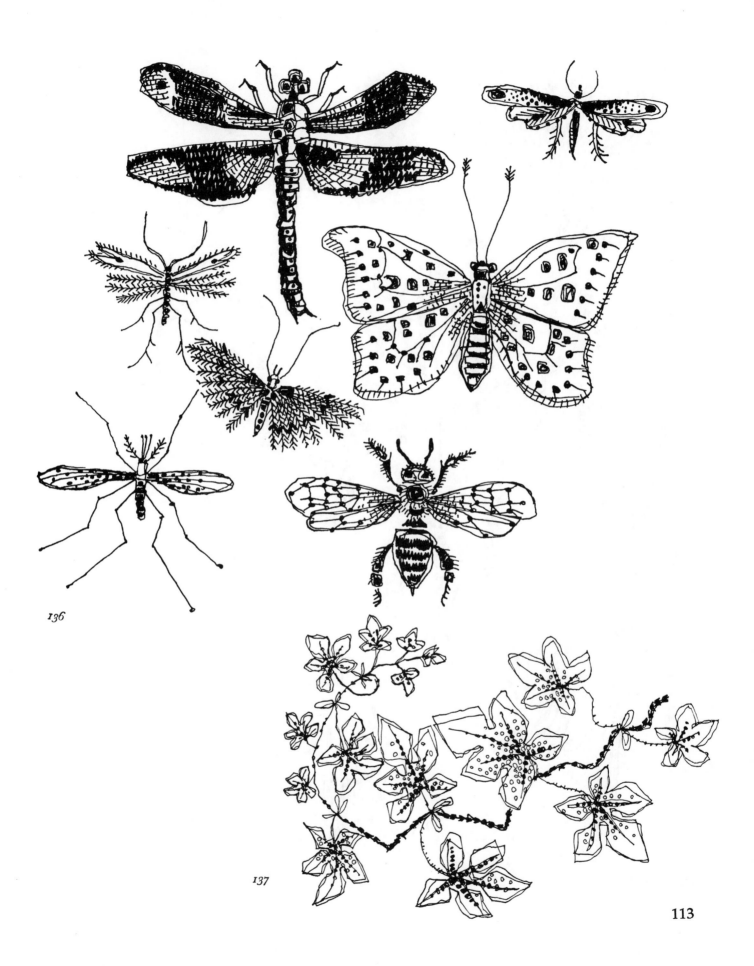

136

137

138

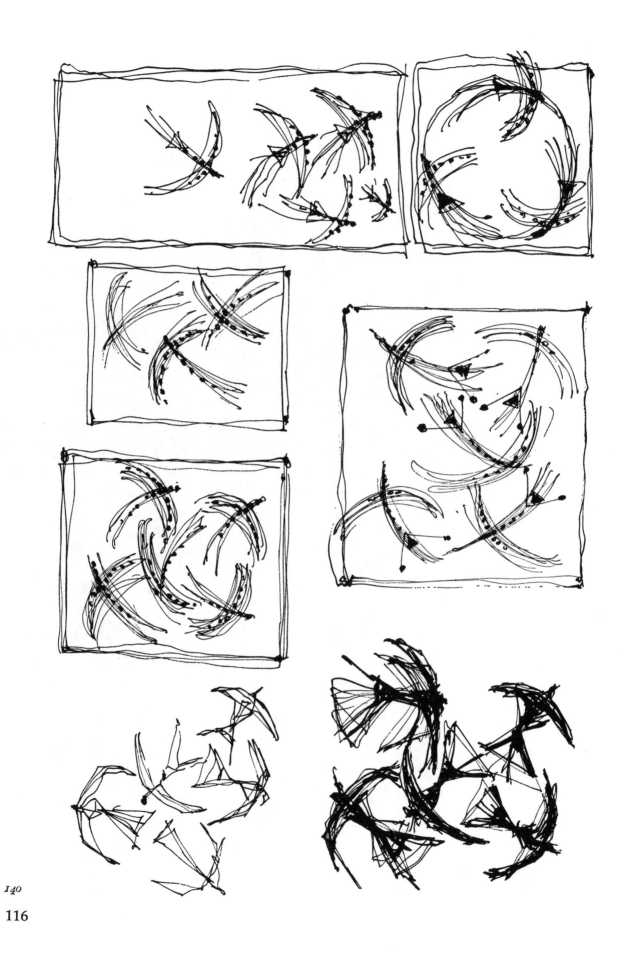

Geometric patterns

SIMPLE beaded repeating patterns can be very easily made. On a piece of soft material place a red bead against a white bead, and another red bead beyond that; push them close together, leave a small space, and set up a row consisting of one red, one white and one red bead.

The line can be thickened by making two or three similar rows one below the other:

or altered entirely by putting the white beads outside the red ones:

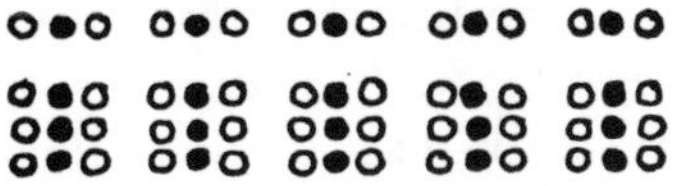

and finally by removing some of the red and then some white beads from these two rows, a series of little triangles is evolved:

When these are rearranged back to back a complicated border pattern is produced:

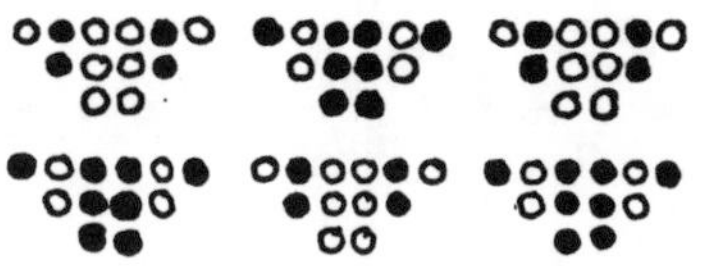

If some bugles are added, all-over repeating patterns can be built up:

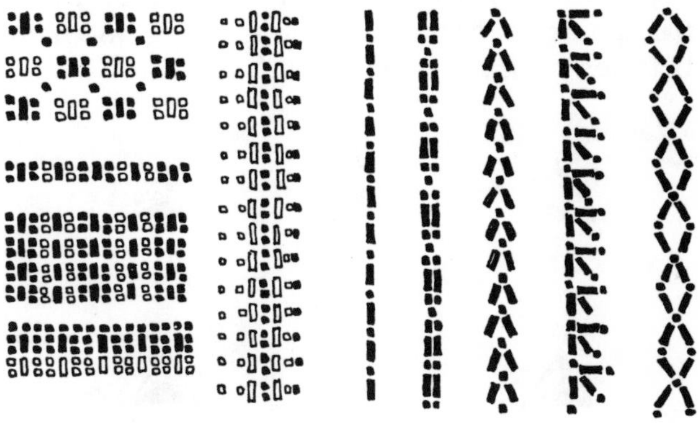

117

All-over repeating patterns that would cover the pocket on a suit, or act as a background to surface stitchery, can also be built up:

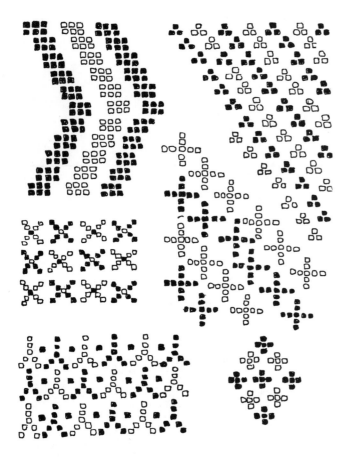

Gather up a small assortment of beads between your fingers—say three different sizes of round beads and a few bugles—and sprinkle them like hundreds and thousands over the triangular beads in the top line to make a Scatter Row.

Stab the largest ones and the bugles in place with pins. This helps to draw attention to the positions into which they have fallen, and also provides an easy way of moving them without disturbing the other beads in the Scatter Row.

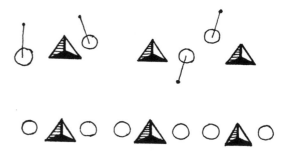

Now consider the largest beads. Where have they fallen? There is one at each end of the Scatter Row; one in the space between the first two triangular beads; and two between the second pair.

Pick up these beads on their pins and transfer them to corresponding positions on the row below. Neaten the line and make it regular by adding another bead between the first pair of triangular beads. We are now making a Pattern Row.

More complicated patterns envolving beads of different shapes and sizes can be made in the following way:

Fold a piece of material, preferably woollen, so that it makes a soft pad about five inches square. Tack or chalk two parallel lines across it approximately two inches apart. Place three triangular beads on each line allowing one inch between them.

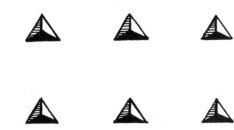

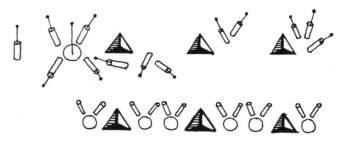

Now look back at the bugles. Four of them have fallen round a large bead on the extreme left of the Scatter Row. This suggests a star arrangement to try out on the Pattern Row. The result is dull and obvious. However, by taking away the bugles on the lower side we see that those above have two good reasons for being left there (i) they lie parallel to the sides of the triangular beads and therefore emphasise them, and (ii) they act as pointers to the large beads. They are, in fact, essential to the pattern.

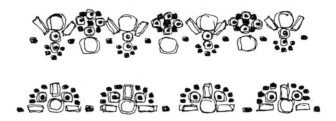

Building up patterns in the same way.

Now try the smaller beads in various positions. The tendency is for them to make the Pattern Row look spotty. If one is placed below each large bead they will act as pendants to them, and will balance the bugles above. Thus they also have two reasons for being there.

Smocking dots will help to keep the lines of beads straight when the time comes to sew them in place.

Now for the smallest beads. Pick up a few in your fingers and sprinkle them over the Pattern Row. Perhaps a line of them along the bottom would give it unity, but this does not seem right.

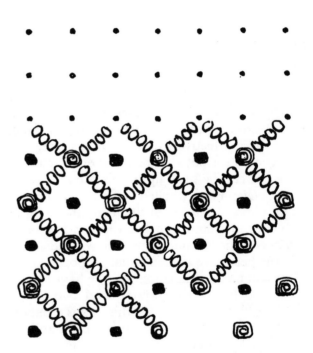

A few have been caught, perhaps in the angles made by the bugles; only very small beads could have fitted in here. Suddenly you see how empty the whole pattern was without them; they have found their proper place and the whole Pattern Row is complete.

Beads on net

STILL using the same simple building-up technique, a pattern can be made up that will occupy a much greater area than the border patterns of the previous chapter. Beads like room in which to move themselves about and with careful planning comparatively few beads can be made to fill effectively quite a large space.

A geometric pattern for an evening stole of black net can be built up in this way.

Materials: Pins, woollen 'palette', a sheet of graph paper 8 squares to the inch, and roughly 12 inches long and 8 inches wide. A few black and crystal beads and a few yellow beads.

If the beads are used in equal proportions, the effect will be very monotonous. We have only to place two black, two crystal, and two yellow beads on the 'palette' to see this. Six is a tedious number, but try adding a seventh bead and the group immediately becomes more interesting. The element of surprise has been introduced, the unexpected lack of uniformity jolts the eye, and what was dull and repetitious takes on some animation and life. Monotony can be guarded against by scattering, quite deliberately, an unequal number of beads on the 'palette'—say two-thirds black, one-third crystal, and only a tiny sprinkling of the yellow.

Begin the pattern by arranging, near the top of the graph paper, a row of beads consisting of one black, one crystal, one black, and so on.

Leave two squares between each bead. In the illustrated pattern three more rows were laid down immediately below in the following order:

2nd row: leaving three squares below each bead in the first row, lay out a row of black beads;

3rd row: leaving four squares below each of these, lay out a row consisting of one crystal, one black, one crystal, and so on;

4th row: leaving three squares, lay out a row of crystal beads.

● ○ ● ○ ● ○ ● ○ ● ○ ●

● ● ● ● ● ● ● ● ● ● ●

○ ● ○ ● ○ ● ○ ● ○ ● ○

○ ○ ○ ○ ○ ○ ○ ○ ○ ○ ○

Together these four rows make up a framework that can be enlarged upon, and from which other rows can directly descend.

Once the process of building up begins, the problem of balance arises. Commencing from the first rather scant rows in which one, five, or nine beads go to make up a block, there should be a gradual increase in the number of beads used in each row; so that in terms of weight, the size of the pattern steadily increases, and larger and larger blocks are developed.

When the blocks have reached a desirable maximum both in the number of beads used and in the area they cover, the whole pattern can be reversed, turned upside-down upon itself so that there are two base lines butting against each other. This will make a strong centre core to the pattern which now balances both vertically and horizontally.

Now take one of the vertical patterns bead by bead, and spread it out on another sheet of graph paper, in such a way that more and more squares show between them, and they are no longer a self-contained, closely packed block.

When you are satisfied, make a little key by which to identify the colours of the beads; say a black spot for the black, a circle for the crystal, and a cross for the yellow; and then, removing one bead at a time, mark up the graph paper according to this key. When all the beads have gone, you will be left with the pattern. Make sure that the marks are dark enough or they will not show through the net.

Fix the graph paper to a piece of thin card, and lay the centre fold of the net along the centre line of the pattern. Tack the net firmly over the card. 'The beads', to quote *The Dictionary of Needlework*, Caulfield and Saward (1882) 'are then threaded singly upon fine black silk, and sewn upon the net. Each bead should be passed to the end of the thread before stitching, this prevents tiny pieces of thread from showing beyond the holes, a sure proof that the work has been done by an inexperienced hand'. The thread cannot be ended off until the net is removed from the card.

Two needles are required for a slightly more painstaking way of sewing beads to net. Small groups of beads are threaded over the first needle laid along the pattern, and couched down with the second which then passes through the next beads so that no untidy stitches are left behind.

On the principle that an even number can be dull, work an odd number of these motifs across the ends of the stole. This is best achieved by working the first one on the centre fold. Then build outwards from the centre towards the edges, either by arranging three or four motifs at equal distances from each other on either side of it; or perhaps by thickening the centre so that it consists of three contiguous blocks, and making only one or two beyond it.

Finally a narrow hem should be turned down on the sides of the stole and tacked in place. It can be almost invisibly secured by stitching black beads along it; or by decorating it with one of the first simple border patterns described in the previous chapter.

The ends of the stole can be finished with a beaded fringe, but it is worth while to consider the possibility of using one of the long fine silk fringes.

The double curve motif

TO design a pattern to fill a given space is one of the trickiest problems posed by any method of embroidery, but a brief study of the beaded patterns devised by the Indian tribes of Labrador, the Maritime Provinces of Canada, New Brunswick, and Maine, show us how satisfactorily it can be dealt with.

The origin of what has come to be called the Indians' *double curve motif* is obscure. The designs are not peculiar to embroidery but were also incised on bone, etched on bark, and carved on wood. They consist of a series of brackets arranged in different positions—sometimes on end, sometimes back to back, and sometimes upright—but in such a way that they always produce a number of enclosed areas on which beads are scattered according to the taste or intention of the embroiderer.

The illustrations show three arrangements of what appear to be substantially similar motifs, that have been used to fill three very differently shaped areas on a child's cap, on a collar, and on a hood.

The way in which the pattern varies to meet whatever shape it is required to fill, depends on the method used for sewing the beads, which are, in fact, only threaded on cotton, and couched in long, continuous lines. The point of the double curve is that it allows the string of beads to double back upon itself, to return along the line it has already travelled over, and to pass on to another part of the design. In this way the motifs are all linked together, and flow in and out of each other, never becoming scrappy or disconnected.

The pattern on the cap is worked throughout in one string of beads. The direction it takes can be seen by following the arrows on the diagram 146(*b*). On the longer patterns the ends are usually hidden in the 'horns', and the motifs so interlocked that there are only two or three places left incompleted by one thread.

On the scarlet collar the white beaded brackets have been fitted into the angles at either end; and on the hood, where three different patterns have been used to cover the entire surface, they have been adapted to the awkwardly shaped area contained between the straight base line, the sloping peak, and the irregular sides, the longest of which is curved to fit the shape of the head. This is a very attractive garment to make for a child to wear in the winter.

It was customary for additional beads of various colours to be arranged around the brackets. These were not stitched individually, as one might expect, but in twos. Thus a group of four beads was made by crossing two stitches, on each of which two beads were threaded.

To the Indian, the way in which the brackets and beads were arranged could be highly significant, and they were used with serious purpose on the regalia worn during important tribal ceremonies. For example, the white beaded designs on the black cape that was draped around the shoulders of one of the officers during the ritual connected with the election of a new Algonquin chief, have been interpreted as representing the different villages and families gathered together by ties of friendship (144) (a); the place of mourning itself, and the leaders, headmen, and members of the dead chief's family, on whom the mourning rested until a new chief was chosen (144)(b). Amongst the Mohawks the scrolls or curves were emblematic of the horned head-dresses worn by chiefs, and so the patterns are sometimes referred to as *horned trimmings*.

The way in which the brackets found their way into the later, floral patterns of the same tribes, is shown in fig. 147.

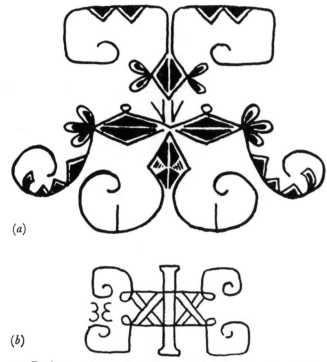

(a)

(b)

144 Designs on ceremonial cloak used in mourning for a dead chief which represent (a) the villages and families concerned and (b) the place of mourning, headmen of the tribe, and the relatives of the dead man
Drawn from 'The Double Curve Motif in Algonkian Art', F. G. Speck 1913

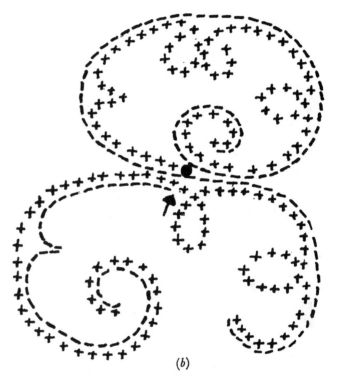

(b)

145(a) The double curve motif arranged to fit into the pointed ends of a collar   Micmac Indians, British Museum
(b) Method of working

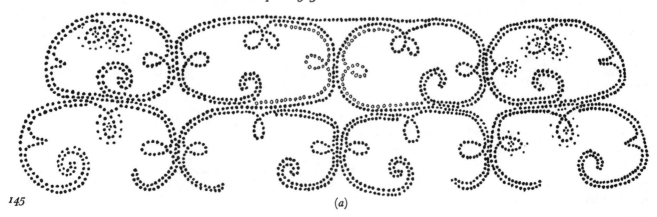

145   (a)

(a)

(b)

146 *The double curve motif on a child's cap*

British Museum

(a) *Detail of the pattern*
(b) *Method of working*

147 *Two designs showing how the 'brackets' of the double curve motif intruded at a later date into the floral patterns of the American Indians*

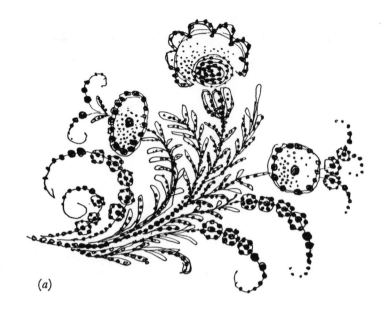

(a)

149

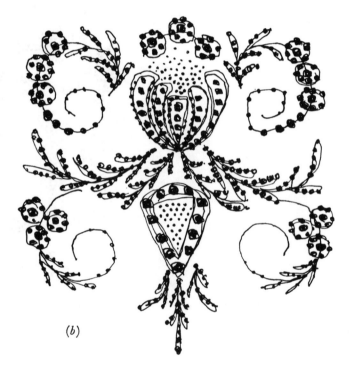

(b)

150

151

152 (a) and (b) Whitework patterns

149–51 Drawings from mosaics

Part V Beading methods

Bead embroidered bags

A BEAD embroidered bag is never completely out of fashion. It is always unusual enough to be attractive and many old ones have interesting associations and histories.

Some time ago I was shown a bag that was worked on canvas with beads instead of wools or silks. On one side a tough, busy little paddle steamer was sailing through a sea of milk-white beads, with three disproportionately large flags and a plume of coal black smoke waving behind (169 and 170). There is a photograph of a similar bag in *The Priscilla Beadwork Book*, from which I discovered that this purse was originally called *The Smyrna Bag*, because it was brought from Smyrna many years ago. It is, of course, just possible that this may be true, but when dealing with beads nothing should be taken for granted. In another old magazine I found an advertisement which casts grave doubts on this story.

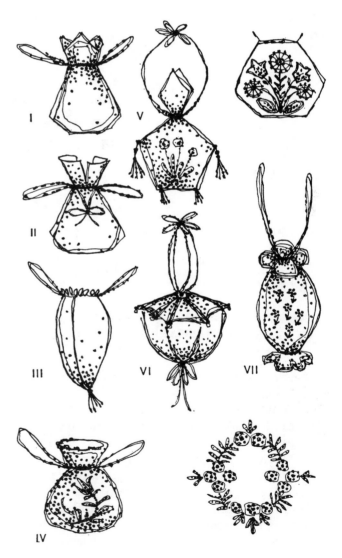

168 (i) *The Parisian Ridicule (1830–35)*
  (ii) *The Richleau Bag, designed by a Parisian milliner in 1835 and named after the street in which she lived*
  (iii) *The Seymour Bag*
  (iv) *The Brown Clayton Bag named after General Brown Clayton who was created Prince of the Holy Roman Empire in recognition of his services to the Papal see after the Peninsular War*
  (v) *The Mitre Bag*
  (vi) *The Chinese Bag (1835) is always illustrated with ladies in walking costume*
  (vii) *The Princess Sophia Bag*

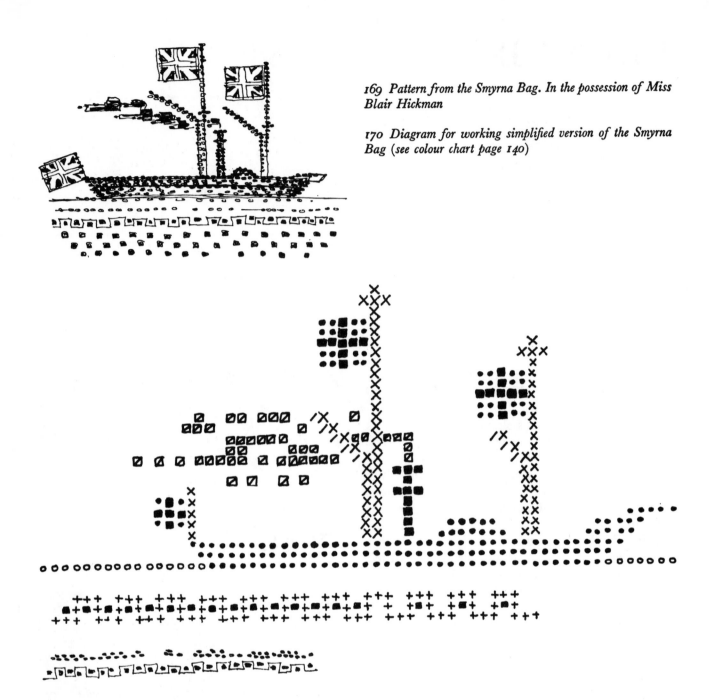

169 *Pattern from the Smyrna Bag. In the possession of Miss Blair Hickman*

170 *Diagram for working simplified version of the Smyrna Bag (see colour chart page 140)*

'Smyrna' it shows was at one time synonymous with 'Oriental', and Berlin Wool Repositories and Fancy Drapers supplied 'Smyrna cotton, coloured designs, design books, Smyrna staffs, colour cards and instructions' for making 'Home-knit Oriental (Smyrna) Rugs from Oriental (Smyrna) Wool'. It seems likely, therefore, that neither the bag nor the pattern was actually made in this remote Turkish city, and that the Victorians—because plainly it is of a date prior to 1900—were only continuing their usual prac-

tice of giving names to the embroidered bags which came and went with the fashions. At one time the *Melon* bag was 'in', the *Chinese* bag was 'out'; there was the *Parisian Ridicule* of the 1830s which later became the *Reticule*; the *Princess Sophia* bag, the *Brown Clayton* bag, the *Richleau* bag, and so on; and the *Smyrna* bag probably got its name because the pattern was adapted from the then popular Oriental or Smyrna work rugs. The beads were purely a novel addition.

128

171 Motif and border pattern from a small beaded purse worked in beads on canvas and sold as a tourist souvenir in 1965. Many of these are made in the Far East, rates of pay being calculated per thousand beads sewn

■	Red		
●	Blue	O	White
/	Orange	+	Green
×	Yellow	☑	Black

When making a beaded bag on canvas choose first the frame on which it is to be mounted. This establishes the shape that the bag will take, and the design must be arranged to fit within this area. When it has been painted on the canvas, work a row of cross stitch in heavy silk or cotton just outside the outer edge of the bag. This holds the beads at the outline and covers the canvas where the edges will finally be overcast together. Cut the canvas an inch or more outside this and apply it to a piece of strong linen which has been mounted on a small embroidery frame. Cut away the linen from behind the bag and tighten the work. If the frame is large enough, both sides of the bag and the gusset can be framed up together.

Resist the temptation to work the design before the background or the result will be disastrous. *It cannot be too often emphasised that beading on canvas must be worked from left to right.* When each row is finished, secure the thread and begin another row at the left hand side. If this procedure is not followed the surface will be rough and disorganised. The beads and canvas must correspond in size and several experiments should be made before the final choice is settled. Too many different beads are available to make practical advice on this reliable. A strong thread is necessary, but this again depends on the beads and canvas selected. It should, however, always be waxed. Almost any canvas work pattern is suitable for this type of bag, and any counted thread pattern can be worked in beads on canvas or even-weave material as, for example, the little bag that belonged to Constanze Mozart and is exhibited in the Mozart Museum in Salzburg.

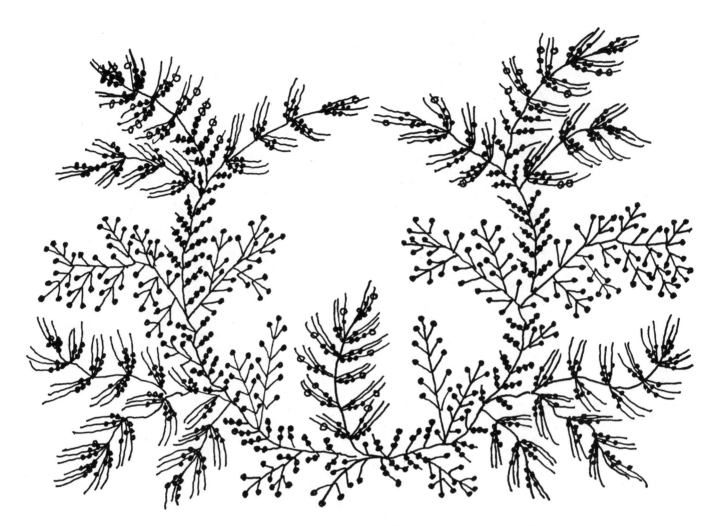

172 Pattern worked on green silk on a bag thought to have been owned by the wife of Captain Cook
Gawthorpe Foundation, Burnley, Lancs.

Constanze, after the death of Mozart, married von Nissen, and it was as Constanze von Nissen that she owned and used this delightful object. It is worked on fine linen canvas in a geometric pattern counted on the thread. The short rows converge towards the centre of the bag and consist of small red triangles followed by three dark green stitches, each of which was originally topped with a gold bead. There were two rows of gold beads between the pattern rows, and although the bag is well-worn enough remain to show how the pattern went (174).

Another type of beaded bag belonged, it is believed, to the wife of the explorer, Captain James Cook. At any rate, it came from her family and is in the collection at the Gawthorpe Foundation, Burnley, Lancashire. The design is charming: a delicate affair worked on green silk in white, crystal and grey beads. They are extremely small and the effect is delightful. Before starting work it is advisable to make a few experiments to discover how these three kinds of bead can be combined, and how they can best be disposed so that each contributes its infinitesimal tone to the whole design (172).

Today, the fashion for what was called Anglo-Indian embroidery is forgotten; it raged for a period and vanished away, but beaded bags

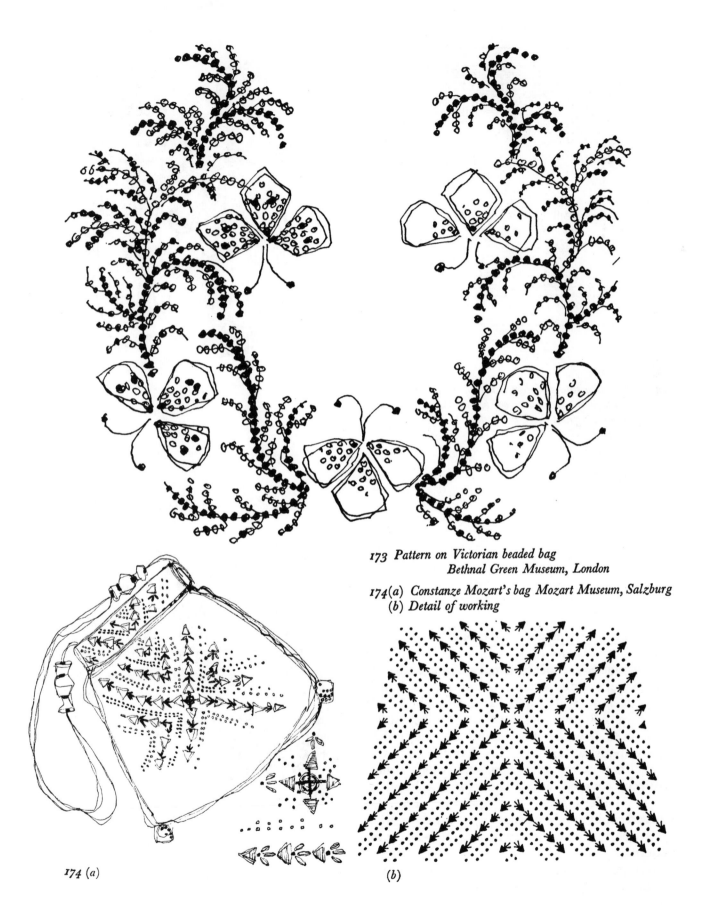

173 *Pattern on Victorian beaded bag*
Bethnal Green Museum, London

174(a) *Constanze Mozart's bag Mozart Museum, Salzburg*
(b) *Detail of working*

174 (a)

(b)

176

175–6 Bag with similar design to the Mozart Bag with embroidered figure on reverse side on which beads, the same as those used on the front, have been added to make a necklace and head band

177 Anglo-Indian embroidery. Detail of beaded pattern

made in this manner do occasionally crop up in old cupboards and inherited hoards. They were easily made, the beads simply being added to the large, gaudily printed cotton handkerchiefs or neckcloths which were, as a rule, obtainable only in country towns or on market stalls, though 'a few of better quality can be had at fancy shops' we are told. The handkerchief was first lined with soft linen and then almost entirely covered with beads (or stitchery) of every shade and colour. Spangles and gold thread could also be added (177), and the worker was free to follow her own taste, it being considered by no means necessary that both sides of the pattern should correspond in colour or type of bead.

132

× Yellow
/ Dark Orange
V Dark Red
● Orange
■ Black
* Blue
+ Light Green
△ Dark Green
O White

178 Tiny beaded purse with pinchbeck mount
In the possesion of the author

(a) Detail of working

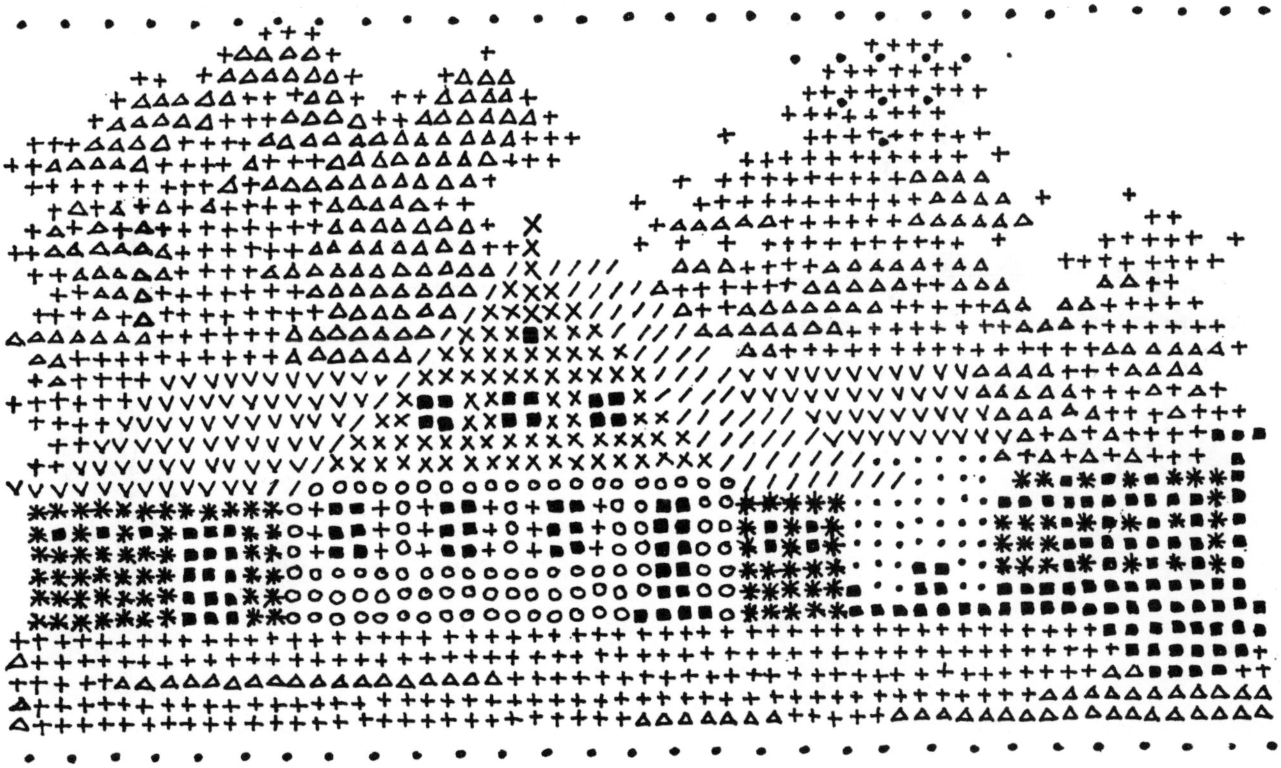

(a)

Because the several beaded bags discussed in the previous pages were all made by embroidery methods, that is to say, the beads were attached directly to the surface of the material with needle and thread, we must now consider the thousands of bags into which beads were introduced not as an afterthought to enrich the fabric, but as an integral part of the material itself, being put into it while it was actually in process of production. In other words, bags that were made by weaving, knitting, netting or crochet techniques. (179)

Originally bags and purses were very small indeed; more like detached pockets, which in fact they were, than anything else. They were carried by both men and women, and strange as it seems, were sometimes considered a sufficiently important possession to be mentioned in a will.

Some were drawn in at the mouth with thinly twisted cords or ribbons; others were stretched on short metal rods, the ends of which might be prettily jewelled; some were mounted on

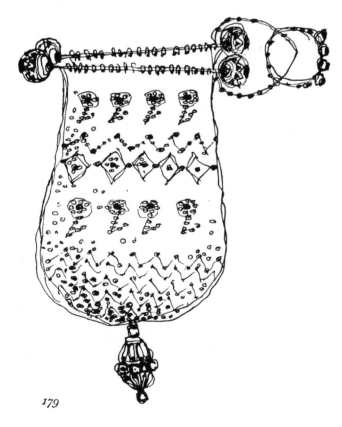

179

180 *Jane Austen's stocking purse*

180

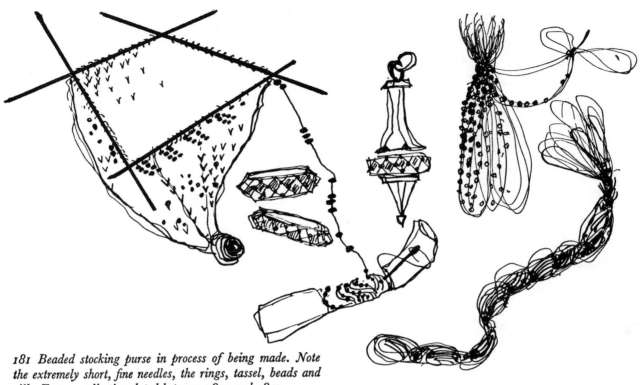

181 Beaded stocking purse in process of being made. Note the extremely short, fine needles, the rings, tassel, beads and silk. From a collection dated between 1830 and 1840
Platt Hall Museum, Manchester

expensive and elaborate pinchbeck or steel frames; and many were closed by one or more circular metal slides. The latter are specially associated with the long, floppy purses that we know best as miser bags or stocking purses, entry into which was gained through a slot left down the centre of the bag during working. One end was usually rounded, and had a single tassel, while the other had square corners and two tassels, the supposition being that coins of different denominations could be kept in either end, making it less troublesome, in the dark recesses of a sedan chair, to find the correct fare for paying the bearers. But whatever the date, shape, or purpose of any of these bags, they were all at one time or another, decorated with beads.

Most ladies possessed several bags. Jane Austen, for example, owned not only the stocking purse (180) with its metal slides and tassels of steel beads, but also two differently shaped bags, both beaded, which are in the City Museum, Winchester. The patchwork quilt and white work shawl that she worked and which are still in her house in the village of Chawton, Hampshire, show that she was an accomplished needlewoman. Miss Mitford, too, who wrote *Our Village*, had beaded bags and has left us a description of them: 'One is of forget-me-nots in beads', she wrote, 'the other of white chrysanthemums in mother-of-pearl and floss silks, that are each of them exquisite. You can hardly conceive,' she goes on, 'the fashion or passion for embroidering at the moment (1833)'.

The ways of making bags were many and various. There were, for instance, two different kinds of *purse mould* on which they could be worked. Usually they were made of wood, but occasionally of ivory, and they can be found in a number of museum collections. Sometimes people who own them have no idea what they were intended for. One, shaped like a large thimble, had a double row of holes arranged round the open end, through which a needle and thread was passed to make a foundation on which the purse could be made. This was usually worked in a buttonhole stitch, and there-

135

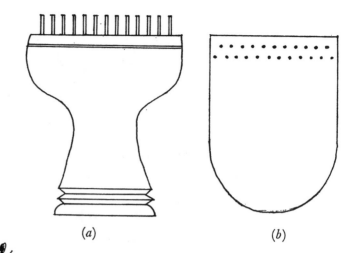

183 Purse moulds   Victoria and Albert Museum, London
(a) the 'moule Turc'
(b) for making a purse 'en feston'

182 Bag being made 'en feston', seventeenth century
Fitzwilliam Museum, Cambridge

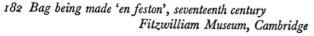

fore the addition of a few beads here and there presented no problem at all. The method which is very old, was known as making a purse *en feston* (182).

The other mould, the *moule Turc*, is a commercial development of the tacks-driven-into-the-end-of-a-cotton-reel type of toy with which most people are familiar from childhood, and once again, beads were easily incorporated into the work as it progressed. In this case the difficulty was, of course, that one could not see what was happening to the pattern as it developed.

Close examination of half a dozen knitted or crocheted bags is enough to convince us how fine and even the work had to be; all the old instruction books insist on this standard of excellence, or else the bags became shapeless and shabby. They recommend sizes 17 or 18 knitting needles, and Mary White tells us that her grandmother used broom wire from a neighbouring factory, as she found it impossible to get needles that were fine enough to satisfy her. A special purse silk was obtainable, and when a purse was finished it was usually put on to an appliance called a *purse stretcher* to settle the stitches.

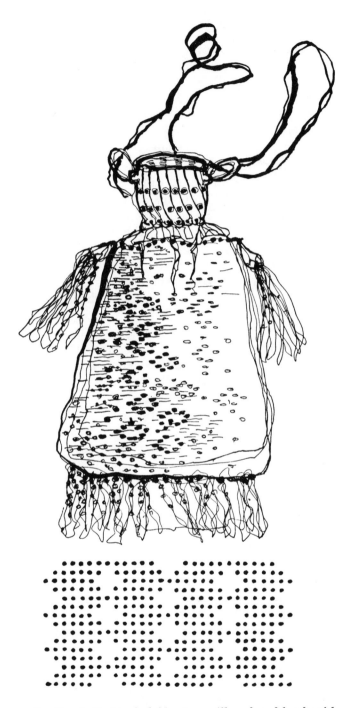

185

186

184 Bag knitted in dark blue purse silk and steel beads with detail of pattern   In the possession of the author

187

185-7 Three pastoral scenes from bags
In the possession of Miss Blair Hickman

137

If the beads were all one colour, it was simple; they were threaded on the purse silk and pushed up as required; but if the design was multi-coloured the beads had to be strung in precisely the right order, and one mistake threw the whole pattern into complete confusion. We are unlikely today to want to knit large crimson roses into our handbags, or pastoral scenes involving a cloudy sky, a figure or two, some animals, a cottage, a bridge, a stream, a mossy bank, and a complexity of shadows, but this was exactly what women in more leisurely days loved to do, and then threading became a matter of patience and immense concentration. When we see what very delicate beads were woven, knitted, or crocheted into just such patterns, we can only marvel at the endurance and dexterity of our ancestors; and it is hardly surprising that they were often as reluctant to share the secrets of their favourite patterns, as to disclose the ingredients of their recipes.

These very human little prides and jealousies were sometimes carried to considerable lengths as a story told by Alice Morse Earle in her book *Two Centuries of Costume in America* (1903) shows:

In one New England town Matilda Emerson reigned as queen of bag-makers; her patterns were beyond compare; and one of a Dutch scene with a windmill was the envy of all who beheld it. She was a rival of Ann Green for the affections of the minister, a solemn widower, whose sister kept house for him and his three motherless children. Matilda gave the parson's sister the written rules for a wonderful bead bag which displayed when finished, a funereal willow tree and urn and grass-grown grave, in shades of grays and purple and white on a black ground; a properly solemn bag. But when the parson's sister essayed to knit this trapping of woe, it proved a sad jumble of unmeaning lines, for Ann Green had taken secretly the rules from the knitter's work-box, and changed the pencilled rules in every line. When the hodge-podge appeared where orderly symbols of gloom should have been seen, the sister believed that Matilda had purposely written them wrong in order to preserve her prestige as a bag-knitter; and she so prejudiced her brother that he turned coldly from Matilda and married, not Ann, but a widow from another town. Ann tormented herself and her New England conscience until she revealed her wickedness to poor Matilda, whose reinstatement in the parson's esteem could not, however, repay her loss of his affections.

Matilda's design can perhaps be compared with the weeping willow tree worked in beads on a sampler made by Elizabeth Harrison in 1837 in memory of Princess Charlotte (188).

Beaded bags are not yet collectors' pieces. They have never been seriously studied, and in my experience, even those who do collect them seldom, if ever, trouble to find out the stories that may lie behind them. It is by no means too late to start building up a small, discriminating collection. It is not an expensive hobby; bags lie about week after week on white elephant stalls and are everlastingly turning up in jumble sales. More often than not, friends are only too happy to part with those they have kept, or which they have inherited and are therefore reluctant to throw away. With care and patience they can often be dated or documented, and even if the bag itself is not worth saving, it will provide a useful supply of beads of all shapes and sizes and colours.

188 Weeping willow tree worked in beads on a sampler made by Elizabeth Harrison in 1837 in memory of Princess Charlotte who, the tombstone announces 'Died November 6 1817 aged 22'

Beaded trimmings

ONE of the forgotten trimmings that beads bring to mind is the *galon*. Variously spelt, this trimming appears frequently on the seventeenth-century haberdashers' trade cards as 'shoe gallooms, shoe lace and breed,' 'galoons, ferrets and every kind of silk bindings', 'silk and statute galloons', and so on; while at the same time one of the cries to be heard in the Paris streets was '*Vieux galons, vieux habits*'. The word is, in fact, derived from the French verb *galloner*, to dress the hair with gold bands or ribbons, and by the late Victorian period we find instructions for making beaded galon ornaments occurring in many publications. Designs were the same as those used for cutwork. They were traced on to a strong linen or cotton foundation, and the embroiderer worked over the outlines in a close chain stitch, slipped the beads on to a long thread, and couched them down—each one separately—completely covering the spaces between the lines of chain stitch. When this was done, paste was spread thinly and evenly on the back of the work; a sheet of tissue paper was pressed down over this with a cloth so that it adhered to every part of the embroidery, and it was set aside under weights until dry. Later, with a pair of sharp pointed scissors, the galon was cut from its background and emerged as a detached motif or medallion that could be applied to a bodice, skirt or mantle.

Medallions made by threading beads on wire were also a fashionable form of ornament. A simple example is made from a yard of wire and beads of two different colours, one dark, the other light. It can be elaborated as desired but the first stage is made like this: Thread two dark beads, one light, two dark, one light, two dark, one light, two dark, one light. Fasten this into a ring by winding the short end two or three times around the long end close to the last bead. In the second row there are thirteen beads on each loop—six dark, one light, and six dark—then the wire passes through the next light bead on the left in the previous row, thus making a loop. When the complete circuit has been made, the end of the wire passes up through the first six dark beads and one light bead in the first loop, and seven dark beads, one light, and seven dark are strung. The wire next passes through the first light bead on the left in the previous row. Care should be taken not to twist the wire, and work should continue in this way, ending with four loops of nineteen dark beads (191).

A *tassel*, slipped through a loop, was probably one of the earliest forms of decorative fastening. Over five hundred years ago they were being imported from the Continent by the London merchants, and, like galons, were amongst the stock carried by haberdashers. The Victorians loved them dearly and festooned themselves

189 *Galon drawn from 'Weldon's Practical Beadwork'*

190 *Tassell design from 'Weldon's Pattern Book'*

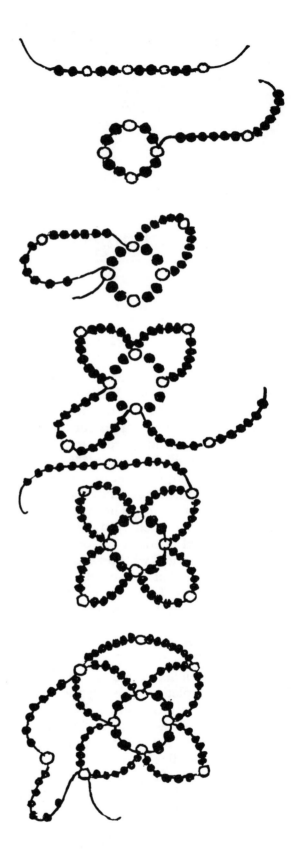

191 *Working instructions for a medallion*

with their swaying glitter, wearing them either singly or looped together with long, complicated beaded chains. For a number of years they were made chiefly of jet and the following pattern was originally made in bright jet beads in two sizes. The head of the tassel is prepared first, the *drops*, or pendants, being added later. Once, there were special wooden moulds made for this purpose but nowadays one has usually to make use of a large wooden bead instead. It should be covered with silk to match the beads, and the thread attached to one end. The needle then passes through to the other end of the mould, sufficient beads to stretch up the side of the mould to the top are threaded, and the needle passes again down through the centre. This process is repeated until the mould is completely covered in lines of beads, which must set evenly or the appearance of the tassel will be ruined. To make the drops, slip eight beads on to a long thread, push them to the middle, and pass the needle through the first two to make a little loop. Make four of these loops taking care that they are all close together. * Pass both ends of the thread through a slightly larger bead, and divide the threads again, slipping six beads on to each. Then pass both threads through one bead. Make four loops again, two on each thread, but put on ten beads instead of eight, and pass both threads through one instead of through two beads. Continue in this way and repeat from * until there are three sets of loops and three large beads. Finally, thread four beads on each thread and knot the ends firmly together. This finishes one drop, of which two are required. To fix them to the body of the tassel, draw the thread through the mould; thread twelve beads on three of the threads and twenty on the fourth, and take the threads back through the mould to the top end of the tassel, and there fasten them off firmly. The longer of these loops in particular must be fastened securely as it is to hold the weight of the tassel when it is in use (190).

There were also *beaded gimps* used for trimming dresses, mantles, bonnets or caps which are included in Godey's articles on *Bead and Bugle Work* of 1854. The first pattern is worked in black bugles and crystal beads of which he says 'an ounce of the former and a bunch of the latter will make a couple of yards of trimming'.

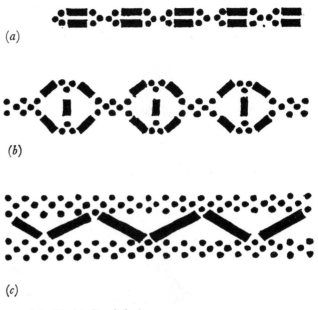

(a)

(b)

(c)

192 (a) (b) (c) Beaded gimps

He threads two needles, knots the ends together, and pins them to a heavy cushion, then threads a bead, a bugle and a bead on one strand; a bead, a bugle and three beads on the other; passes the first strand through the last two beads of the second in a downward or parallel direction; draws the work up to the end, and repeats the process (192(a)).

Another pattern, worked in grey bugles and crystal beads begins in the same manner by attaching two threads to a cushion, and goes on:

Thread a bead on one strand and two beads on the other, cross the first strand through the second bead on the other; draw it up; again thread a bead on one strand and two upon the other, and cross the first strand through the last bead on the second one; thread a bead, a bugle and a bead upon one strand, and a bead, a bugle, two beads, a bugle and a bead upon the other, and cross the first strand through the last bead, bugle and bead upon the second; draw the work up; thread a bead, a bugle and a bead on one strand, and a bead, a bugle and two beads on the other, and cross the first strand through the last two beads on the second. Work a diamond in beads by threading one on one strand, and two upon the other, and crossing the first strand through the last bead on the second; then recommence the large diamond composed of

141

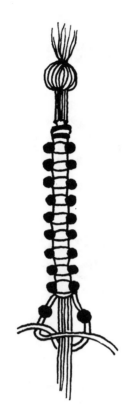

193 Solomon's knot

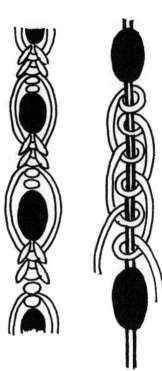

194 Macramé's knot

beads and bugles, and thread it as before directed (192(b)).

Godey also makes a number of composite gimps which are completed in two journeys. First he makes two lengths of diamonds by threading a bead on one thread, two on the other, and passing the first thread through the last bead on the second, and lays these in exactly parallel lines on a cushion. He then attaches another thread to the beginning of one of the rows, threads a bugle on it, and passes the thread through the side bead of the third diamond on the opposite line. Another bugle is threaded, and the needle passes through the side bead of the sixth diamond on the opposite line (192(c)). This is repeated until the two lines of diamonds are united.

Beads can be effectively added to a cord when it is being made for a belt, bag handles, a necklace or any other form of decoration by the methods illustrated in figs 193 to 195.

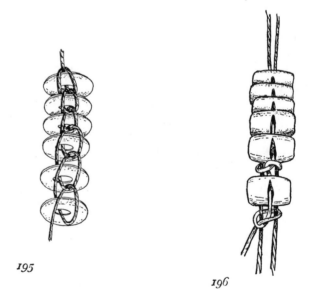

195

196

195 Discoidal beads assembled with a crochet-like stitch

196 Rectangular pieces of shell tied to fibre cords with sinew threads

142

Beaded edgings

BEADED *edgings* are very simple to make and are also amongst the oldest forms of embroidered decorations. Given an awl, a thong, and a supply of shells and the earliest of human beings could make beaded edgings for their skin clothing. The technique was widely practised by the American Indians who used it on both cloth and skin garments including the cap, collar and hood seen in figs 145 to 148. The single-beaded edging and the two-beaded edging are the most frequently used (197, 198). Clearly any number of beads can be attached to an edging in these ways; beads of varying shapes and sizes can be used; drops added, or the threads endlessly entwined until the long, complicated beaded fringes of the last century are evolved.

By making pleats in a piece of material, a number of 'edges' are created and if beads are sewn by one or other of these methods along the 'edge' of each pleat, a large area can be quickly covered with an all-over beaded pattern. A cotton beadwork cloth in the British Museum was worked in this way by one of the Zulu tribes in Africa. Variety was introduced by changing the colour of the beads and so producing a striped effect; about three inches of blue beads being followed by a similar number of white beads, and so on. Repeated row after row, this can be very attractive and as an experiment is well worth further exploration and adaptation.

An unusual and most attractive edge treatment was used by the Victorians to decorate such small objects as pin-cushions and needlebooks. Beads used in this way take on an incredibly rich and jewel-like quality and old beads very often look better than new. A needlebook sewn with steel beads, seed pearls, crystals and one or two gold spangles can be made from a shred of Thai silk (one colour for the outside and another for the lining), black velvet, dark blue satin or taffeta. Cottons or man-made fibres are not suitable. The fabric must be stretched on a frame and on the whole the work is firmer if it is backed.

197 Detail of two-beaded edging

198 Detail of single-beaded edging

143

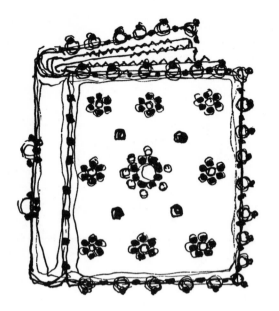

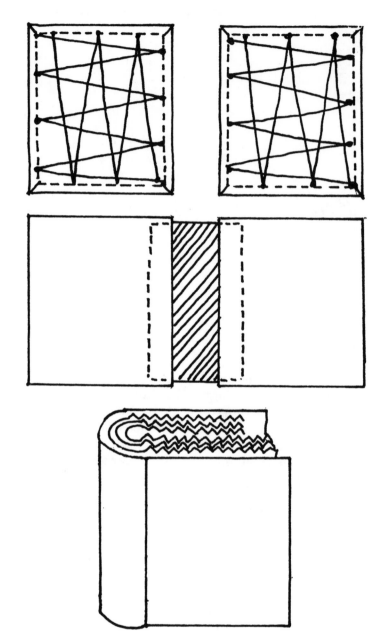

199 Needlebook with beaded edge

Four pieces of cardboard are needed for the covers, say one and a half by two inches; flannel for the pages; and a box of pins.

Place one of the cover cards on the stretched fabric and outline it in tacking stitches. This will be the front of the book. Leaving ample space for turnings between linings, outline another card to make the back.

The simpler the pattern the better the effect.

Outline with pencil one of the covers on a piece of graph paper and work out a tiny pattern, transferring the beads to the squares on the point of a pin or needle. Try balancing a pearl on the centre of a gold spangle, or arranging gold beads and pearls alternately around a crystal; try another circle outside the first in which the beads are spaced less closely together.

It is more effective if the back has a less elaborate pattern than the front; one roundel in the centre perhaps, and a single crystal in each corner. Nothing but trial and error will decide this.

Cut out the beaded covers, leaving good turnings all round, and lace them neatly over two of the pieces of cardboard, taking particular care at the corners.

Lace matching or contrasting fabric over the other two cards, and put one to the front, the other to the back, wrong sides facing inwards. Slip stitch the edges neatly together, except along the spine sides.

To make the spine, cut a piece of material about two inches wide, and a little longer than the cover. Double it in half; stitch the long sides together; and turn it inside out to make a tube. Tuck the ends in and oversew them so that the spine and the covers are exactly the same length. Now work a little geometric pattern along it; perhaps three groups of beads arranged at equal distances apart; or a large central roundel and two smaller ones at the ends; but not just a single line of beads.

To join the front cover to the back, push one side of the spine between the two pieces of card from which the cover is made, and sew the edges down. Repeat this on the other side.

Cut out a supply of flannel pages, pinking the edges, and fit them into the spine. When making needlebooks it is usual to cut the pages double and fold them in half within the spine, but for this little book the effect is often better if the pages are single. In this way a greater number can be fitted in. Place them within the spine, and stitch them into place, passing the needle backwards and forwards as close to the cardboard linings as possible. It does not matter if the stitches are clumsy because they can be hidden by sewing a few beads over them.

Take one of the pins. Slip on to it one tiny bead and then a larger one—say one steel bead and one pearl—and stab the pin into the edge of the book cover. If you are careful you will be able to slide it between the two cardboard linings so that it is firmly held in place. Repeat this all the way round, both back and front.

Perhaps we underestimate the number of small, intimate gifts like this needlebook, that women were once in the habit of making for each other, either to mark an anniversary, or just as an expression of goodwill. Such spontaneous and completely natural gestures have been common to women at all times and in every place. In Africa, for instance, a woman wishing to show warmth or affection towards her neighbour will make an artless little present by mixing sweet-smelling herbs or grasses with clay, which she then shapes between her fingers and decorates with beads or with the red and black seeds of the bead tree (164). Sun-dried, they are given away, or perhaps exchanged, and put to various domestic or personal uses—maybe to grate into washing water to scent it pleasantly.

Knitting with beads

IN her book published in 1857 on needlework, Mrs Henry Owen obviously had no great opinion of knitting, but she did concede that in many of the patterns she gave for it, beads could be effectively substituted for coloured wools—'gold beads tastefully introduced', she says, 'can have a pretty effect'—and certainly it is useful to know how to knit a few beads into a cardigan or jersey.

Work commences by threading the beads on to the wool, and therefore, before either the beads or the wool are purchased, care should be taken to make sure that the wool will pass readily through the hole in the bead. The beads must move easily up and down it, but should be neither so loose that they slip about, nor so tight that they have to be forced.

For knitting, beads are usually threaded in one of the following ways: (i) if the beads are bought in bunches, the cotton on which they are strung is joined to the end of the wool by tying a *weaver's knot* (page 180) over which they can then be passed without further trouble; or (ii) if unthreaded beads are used and the wool is too thick to go through the eye of the needle, a slightly less straightforward course has to be taken. A fine needle over which the beads will pass is threaded with six or seven inches of cotton, the ends knotted together, and the wool pulled through the loop thus formed. The beads are then picked up on the needle and will pass over the cotton and thence to the wool.

After the wool has been wound into a ball, the knitting proceeds in the usual way. When a bead is to be introduced it is pushed up against the back of the needle, and a stitch in plain knitting is made; in this way it is fastened securely into place (200).

The invaluable Mary White, however, proposes a highly idiosyncratic idea for—apparently—knitting beads. It by-passes the method just described and is, she claims, an improvement on the old way of stringing beads according to a pattern. All she does is to knit the garment in the ordinary way, and when it is completed she advises her readers to sew beads as if on canvas wherever they feel they will look most effective.

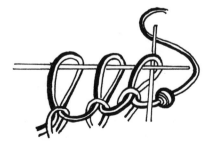

200

202 *Stars were always popular patterns on Victorian bags*

201 *Simple knitted pattern from a very small bag*

Innumerable patterns for knitting beads can be found in old magazines, and although many of the objects that were decorated in this way have long since lost their point and purpose in our daily lives—like a 'sovereign bag', or a collarette of 'best quality black beads with a neckband of black velvet ribbon'—many of them are not to be despised. A basic pattern, for example, is knitted according to these instructions:

Cast on 32 stitches

1st row and every alternate row, knit plain

2nd row: Slip 1, knit 2, knit 5 beaded stitches, knit 3, knit 5 beaded stitches, knit 3, knit 5 beaded stitches, knit 8.

4th row: Slip 1, knit 3, knit 5 beaded stitches, knit 3, knit 5 beaded stitches, knit 3, knit 5 beaded stitches, knit 7.

6th row: Slip 1, knit 4, knit 5 beaded stitches, knit 3, knit 5 beaded stitches, knit 3, knit 5 beaded stitches, knit 6.

8th row: Slip 1, knit 5, knit 5 beaded stitches, knit 3, knit 5 beaded stitches, knit 3, knit 5 beaded stitches, knit 5.

10th row: Slip 1, knit 6, knit 5 beaded stitches, knit 3, knit 5 beaded stitches, knit 3, knit 5 beaded stitches, knit 4.

12th row: Slip 1, knit 5, knit 5 beaded stitches, knit 3, knit 5 beaded stitches, knit 3, knit 5 beaded stitches, knit 5.

14th row: Slip 1, knit 4, knit 5 beaded stitches, knit 3, knit 5 beaded stitches, knit 3, knit 5 beaded stitches, knit 6.

16th row: Slip 1, knit 3, knit 5 beaded stitches, knit 3, knit 5 beaded stitches, knit 3, knit 5 beaded stitches, knit 7.

If, however, we are following the more conventional method it is a wise precaution to knit at first with beads of only one colour, and to attempt only simple repeating patterns in which a mistake is quickly seen and rectified. The whole process is no more difficult than counting any knitting pattern.

'A pair of beaded cuffs with or without frills, for wearing when out walking, or by old ladies who like to wear them in the summer when longer ones are too warm', may not exactly make us reach for our needles, but it is an attractive pattern to use as a trimming.

Cast on 24 stitches

1st row and every alternate row, knit plain

2nd row: Slip 3 stitches as if for purling, from the left to the right hand needle, and pass 4 beads along the wool till they are close to the work, knit 1. The stitches that are slipped in one row must be very loosely knitted in the next, or the work will be drawn out of place and the knitting rendered too tight. Knit 3 beaded stitches, knit 3, knit 5 beaded stitches, knit 3, knit 3 beaded stitches, slip 3, pass along 4 beads.

4th row: Slip 3, pass along 4 beads, knit 1, knit 3 beaded stitches, knit 2, slip 1, pass along 4 beads, slip 2, pass along 5 beads, slip 1, pass along 4 beads, knit 2, knit 3 beaded stitches, slip 3, pass along 4 beads.

Repeat these 4 rows until the trimming is wide enough.

Two other beaded trimmings that were last published over sixty years ago seem worth repeating here, especially as they probably originated many years earlier. A doll in the Bethnal Green Museum, London, is illustrated wearing a very similar type of beading around the neck of her black woollen dress, and is dated 1880 (203). One of the trimmings is knitted lengthwise, and the other across a row of seven stitches. It is interesting to see how very different the results are.

Trimming No. 1. Thread the beads and cast on 150 stitches or any even number required. (No. 16 steel needles are recommended.)

1st row: Knit 2, * push up 7 beads close to the needle, knit 2 and repeat from * to the end of the row. Great care must be taken in this row to knit rather tightly and to keep the loops of beads in the right position.

2nd and every alternate row, knit plain.

3rd row: Knit 1, * push up 7 beads close to the needle, knit 2 and repeat from * to the end of the row where there will be only one stitch to knit.

5th row: Same as the first row.

6th row: Knit plain.

Then knit 4 rows in plain knitting and cast off.

Trimming No. 2. Thread the beads and cast on 7 stitches. (No. 16 steel needles are recommended.)

1st row: Knit plain.

2nd row: Insert the needle in the first stitch as if about to purl, but instead slip it off on to the right hand needle, pass the wool between the first and second stitches to the back of the work, knit 3, slip the next 2 stitches on to the right hand needle without knitting them, push up 7 beads close to the needle at the back of the work, and keeping them firmly in place, knit the last stitch plain.

3rd row: Slip the first stitch as if about to purl, and knit 6 stitches.

Repeat the last 2 rows for the length required. The first stitch in every row being slipped purlwise gives a neat chain-like edge smoother than the edge of ordinary knitting.

For any of these knitted patterns, steel beads were considered to be specially suitable, but contrary to expectation I find that they were manufactured in neither Birmingham nor Wolverhampton, nor is there any evidence to suggest that they were ever made in England, and the records of at least one London bead importer show that their supplies were obtained from France.

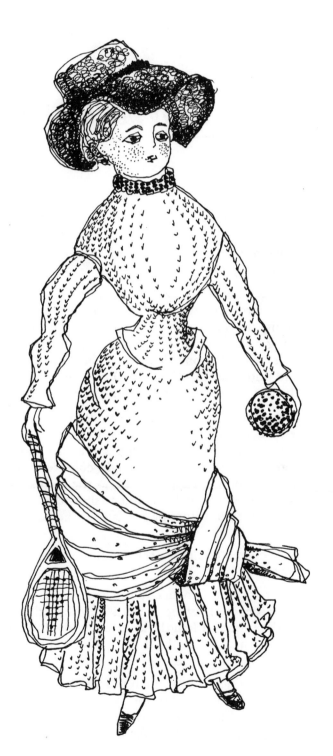

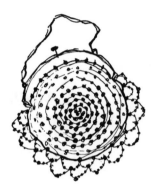

204 *Crocheted bag*

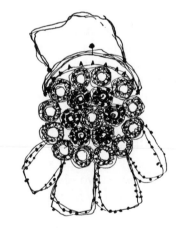

205 *Tatted bag*

203 *Doll dressed for tennis with high beaded collar, c. 1880*
Bethnal Green Museum, London

Crochet, netting and tatting with beads

UNDER the heading *Ornamental Needlework* Godey began publishing crochet patterns in 1846, and in the September issue of the *Lady's Book* printed one for *A Star Bottom for a Bag with Beads*. This pattern recurs time and time again in countless small books and magazines and can be used for a number of purposes:

Make a chain of fourteen stitches, join both ends together with crochet, and crochet one plain row all round. In the next row, every other stitch is to be made a seam or dividing stitch, which is done by putting the needle under both loops instead of under one, and making two stitches in the same place—every other stitch being a plain stitch, on which is to be a bead. In the next row, work the seam stitch exactly over the last, which leaves two plain stitches between instead of one: this is to be repeated until eight circles are formed, every plain stitch having a bead on it. Crochet eight rows more, leaving the seam stitch in the same place, but diminish the number of beads by leaving out one bead in each division on each successive circle, so that the last row will have one bead in each division. Then crochet four plain rows, keeping the seam stitch in the same place as before, then one plain row all round without a seam stitch, which forms the bottom of the bag.

A popular beaded bag was made by working double crochet over a fine cord. The method is described by Weldon's as follows:

Thread beads on twist; take some very fine cotton cord and work double crochet over it, slipping up a bead at every stitch; the beads coming on the side of the work farthest from you. Commence with one double crochet and work round and round to the desired size, then fringe with beads and fasten to a frame or clasp.

One should take great pains to hold the work carefully in the hands, as it is apt to twist. The beads should all slant in the same direction. When working with white or light coloured silk, be most careful to keep it clean, as the least soiling when working will be liable to show through, giving unpleasant lines or grey streaks across the work.

A crocheted chain or necklace can be made in this way:

Chain 5, join. Crochet round and round with single crochet, leaving a bead at each stitch, until the required length has been worked. The cord can then be doubled and twisted into an ornamental knot if desired.

Netting is not now a much practised craft but it was once so popular for beadwork that it would be wrong to omit any reference to it, and the following old pattern for a *Gentleman's Long*

Purse in netting is therefore given. It has been selected also because it shows how the purse stretcher mentioned on page 147 was used.

You will find four skeins of netting silk sufficient, and use a No. 15 mesh. Net on a foundation of 76 stitches until your purse is as wide as you wish it. When this is done, net up the sides, sew up the opening, and put it on a purse stretcher. Having left it for a few hours, take it off the stretcher, unstitch the opening, gather up each end, and put on the rings and tassels. The introduction of beads adds greatly to the beauty of this work, and in working bead rows a fine long darning needle must be used instead of the netting needle. The process is as follows: Thread the needle with as much silk as you require for each row; string each bead on the silk you net with, and pass it on to the top of the mesh; then net a stitch and pass the silk under the mesh, and through the bead; after that bring the silk back again under the mesh, and draw the bead with it, leaving the bead on the knot. Patterns in Bead Netting may be copied from Crochet Patterns.

Beads were also added to tatting, and we are told that small irridescent beads look extremely pretty on beaded insertions or edgings. They should be threaded on the silk or cotton and wound on to the shuttle before commencing to tat. A simple pattern can be worked as follows:

Begin by making a loop on the fingers, work in the loop 4 double stitches, push down a bead, 1 picot, 3 double stitches, 1 bead, 1 picot, 4 double stitches, and draw up; reverse, make loop, miss one-twelfth of an inch from the last oval, make 4 double stitches, push down a bead, 1 picot, 3 double stitches, 1 bead, 1 picot, 3 double stitches, 1 bead, 1 picot, 4 double stitches, and draw up; * reverse, make loop, miss one-twelfth of an inch from the last oval, and work 4 double stitches, push down a bead, join to corresponding picot of the first oval, work 3 double stitches, 1 bead, 1 picot, 4 double stitches, 1 bead, 1 picot, 3 double stitches, 1 bead, 1 picot, 4 double stitches, and draw up; reverse, make loop, miss one-twelfth of an inch of thread, and work 4 double stitches, 1 bead, join to picot of second oval, work 3 double stitches, 1 bead, 1 picot, 3 double stitches, 1 bead, 1 picot, 4 double stitches, and draw up. Repeat from * thus forming alternately one oval on the top line and one oval on the lower line.

Part VI Beadwork

Beaded flowers

MOST of the literature of beadwork is buried deeply in magazine articles that are now well over a hundred years old. The instructions they contain are very differently expressed from the concise, clipped, and clearly stated sentences in which present-day patterns are set out, and for this reason they have a certain style and charm of their own. The following directions, for instance, for making beaded flowers and sprays, first appeared in Godey's *Lady's Book* in 1854 and have a persuasive power that is difficult to resist:

Very pretty flowers or sprays may be made of bugles for the decoration of ball-dresses or for wearing in the hair. Black, white, grey, green, purple and pink bugles, well adapted for this purpose, may be obtained at any of the bead and bugle-makers, or retailers; by far the greater part of these are imported from abroad. For flowers we use two sizes, the one about an eighth of an inch in length, or rather better, and the other one-third of an inch long. A bright even-looking bugle large in the tube, should be chosen, and an ounce of each will make a very fair spray. Besides we shall require beads rather larger than a mustard seed—this size is usually solid and is sold in bunches. The other requisites are wire and floss-silk, the wire being chosen to match the colour of the bugles. These covered wires are to be obtained at the artificial flower-makers, and are sold in reels; the green can be bought in knots at the wax-flower makers. The floss silk at any Berlinwork repository. The leaves are made of small bugles. About nine leaves will make a small spray. There are, however, various patterns of bugle leaves, many of which will suggest themselves to anyone practising the work. We will, however, give a cut (i.e. an illustration). For the top loop or point of the leaf, we thread a long bugle, a bead, a long bugle, a bead, a long bugle, a bead, and then another long bugle, and bringing them to the centre of the wire, twist it immediately below them for a quarter of an inch. The two next loops are made each on their separate wire, in like manner, and the two wires are again twisted together for a third of an inch. The second pair of loops, or base of the leaf, are made by threading first a long bugle, and then a bead, then three bugles, and a bead twice, and then a long bugle on each wire, and fixing the loops by a twist to each, and then twisting the two wires together as a stem. When complete, each leaf will require putting into shape.

Bugle flowers are of two kinds, double and single, and are composed of bugles of both sizes, and beads, and look handsomer if finished off with a larger bead, one the size of a pea in the centre.

152

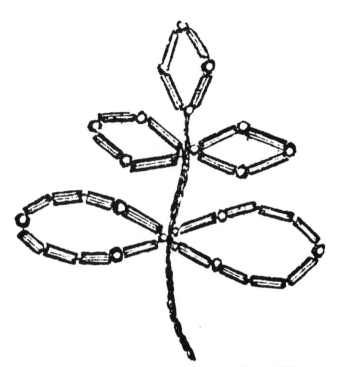

206–7 Diagrams from Godey's Lady's Book Vol. XLIX July–December 1854

Take about three-quarters of a yard of wire, thread on it a bead, a long bugle, seven short bugles, and a long bugle; push these to within two inches of one end of the wire, and then pass the longer end of the wire again through the bead from the outside, inwards, or towards the bugles; draw it up gently and closely, and the first loop petal of the flower is formed. Thirteen loops are required, and each one is made in the same way, the wire being always put a second time through the bead, entering it from the side of the loop last made, and being drawn up closely. These loops or petals stand up and overlay each other; when all are completed, the two ends of the wire are twisted together to form the stem, and the circular, cup-shape of the flower is thus finished up.

When the flower is to be double, a second cup or circle of upstanding loops must be made; but this inner portion contains eleven instead of thirteen petals, and there are but five small bugles instead of seven in each; in all other respects it is exactly similar. The stem is passed down through the centre of the outer cup, and a large bead being threaded on a couple of inches of wire and held in place by a twist of the ends of the wire, is passed through the centre of the cups, and the three twisted wires are wound together into one neat system with floss silk.

207

Single flowers look best small; therefore the inner cup with the central large bead should be used for them. Various fantastic groupings of beads and bugles may be combined to form other flowers, or to simulate buds. We give a cut of one of them which is made of long bugles, short bugles, and beads, threaded on four wires, and arranged in diamonds. About four flowers, two single and two double, a couple of buds, and nine or ten leaves, make a pretty spray, if tastefully grouped and neatly bound together with floss silk. The size we make them of course depends upon the purpose for which they are

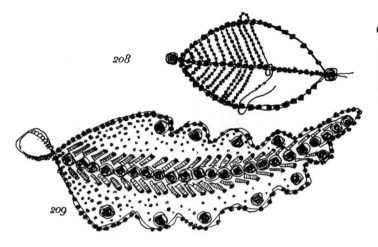

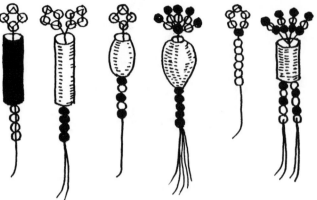

210 Stamens for beaded flowers

required; for looping up a dress, five leaves, a bud, and two flowers will be sufficient.

For mourning, black, white or grey bugles make up very prettily. Green bugles, too, have a very brilliant effect, and elegant sets of sprays or wreaths may be made by following our directions, at a merely nominal price compared with the cost of them were we to order them to be made. Besides, the work itself is a graceful and pretty employment for the fingers, and calls for a certain degree of taste and imagination, and is very suggestive. We therefore recommend it to our readers in full confidence that it will amuse and interest them.

Twelve years later the *Englishwoman's Domestic Magazine* produced a pattern for 'a petal for a candlestick ornament' in which the beads for the outline and the centre vein were threaded on wire, but for filling up the spaces between the beads were threaded on silk (208).

Later still Weldon's *Practical Beadwork* describes 'an elegant leaf for the ornamentation of a lace hat or bonnet' in jet, crystal or pearl beads (209), which is made as follows:

The shape of the leaf itself must be carefully cut out in stiff net, and outlined with black covered wire, the two ends of which, about half an inch long, are left and twisted together to form the stalk. A row of cut jet beads, threaded on wire is sewn all round the edges, the stitches which secure this being taken over the wired edges of the leaf. A large cut jet bead is sewn on each curve of the leaf. Run a line of black cotton to mark the centre of the leaf, from the stalk to the tip, and on each side of this sew on

a row of bugles, so arranged as to start from this centre as fish bones do from the spine. Leave a space of half an inch up the middle between each row of bugles, but put them as closely as possible one over the other. It will be found necessary to put only one row of bugles when within an inch and a half from the tip.

Thread about three dozen of the largest cut jet beads on wire. Twist one end of the wire round the stalk of the leaf, and sew a line of large beads along the centre of the leaf between the two rows of bugles. It will now be seen that the reason why only one row of bugles was sewn near the tip was to gain space for this central string of larger beads. Finish off the end of the wire at the top by pushing it through to the wrong side and sewing it firmly down. Sew a number of smaller beads singly, dotting them about at irregular intervals over the remaining portions of the net, and finally twist a strip of black tissue paper round the stalk of the leaf.

At one time quite a considerable number of people made a livelihood by twisting beads and wire together to make these flowers, sprays, leaves and ornaments; but there was another, more unusual call made upon their work. Beaded funeral wreaths in enormous numbers were required and until very recently were, in fact, still used. They can still be found in remote country cemeteries on the continent, leaning up against wooden crosses and marble headstones, their pansies, forget-me-nots and roses surrounding sad messages and trusting texts. They are very nearly indestructible but their place has been taken in the popular favour by the plastic pinks and yellows and greens of artificial flowers.

Beads on Wire

Christmas Decoration

Thread 9 beads on about 36 inches of fine wire and pass them to the centre.

Bend the wire so that a loop is formed.

Arrange the beads so that they lie neatly side by side, and twist the wires together for one-quarter of an inch.

Separate the wire again and thread 9 beads on each.

Push the beads together and form two more loops; twist the wires together for one-quarter of an inch.

Separate the wires and thread nine more beads; bring them together to make two more loops; twist wires together for one-quarter of an inch. Repeat until there are nine loops on the spray.

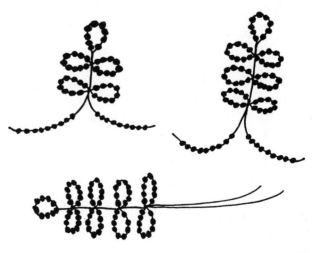

To Make a Candle

Thread three red bugles and five small yellow beads on twelve inches of wire. Push them to the centre and thread one wire through the bugles; attach the candle to the spray twisting the ends of the wire in and out between the eight loops. This will serve to strengthen the spray.

Make four more sprays and candles each with eleven loops; four more with thirteen loops; four with fifteen loops; and four with seventeen loops. Cover a wooden knitting needle with binding and attach one of the smallest sprays immediately below the knob, twisting the four wires protruding from the end around the knitting needle. Arrange the other three small sprays at equal distances around the needle and attach them by twisting their wires. Place the next four sprays (eleven loops) so that they fit into the spaces between the first row of sprays and twist them round the needle about half an inch below. Add the remaining sprays in the same way until the tree is formed. Stitch to the binding if necessary.

Take a long piece of wire and thread it with small crystal beads; attach it below the knob and twist it round the needle to cover the wires. Tuck the end securely out of sight by running it back through four or five beads.

Sew four silver holly leaves and a few red beads or stamens to the knob on top of the knitting needle.

Set the knitting needle in a tiny cactus pot filled with plaster of Paris, *Polyfilla* or some other quick-drying material, so that the tree stands erect. Tie a bow of red ribbon round the pot.

Trim the branches with the smallest round Christmas tree decorations; straighten the candles, and arrange the branches so that they bend downwards and then upwards towards the ends.

156

Bead furniture for a doll's house

Arm Chair

1 On a wire 16 inches long (thread 6 blue beads and cross through the first bead. Three times.)

2 On one of the wires thread 1 blue bead, and with the other cross through it; thread 3 blue beads; the third one must be large enough for 4 wires to go through it. On the other wire thread 2 blue beads, then cross through the third bead.

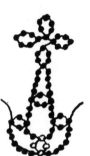

3 On one of the wires thread 9 blue beads and cross through the fifth bead.

4 On the other wire thread 4 blue beads, and pass the wire upwards through the eighth of the 9 beads.

5 On one of the wires thread 6 blue beads and cross through the third bead. Repeat with the other wire.

6 On one of the wires thread 2 blue and 1 white bead; on the other wire thread 2 blue beads and cross through the white bead.

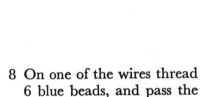

7 On one of the wires thread 2 white beads; on the other wire thread 1 white bead and cross through the second bead.

8 On one of the wires thread 6 blue beads, and pass the wire through the second of the nearest 3 beads. Repeat with the other wire.

9 On one of the wires thread 9 blue beads, and pass the wire through the bead below the 4 beads.

10 On the same wire thread 2 blue beads; on the other wire thread 7 blue beads, and cross through 2 beads and through the next 3 beads.

11 On one of the wires thread 3 blue beads and pass the wire through the middle bead of the 5 next to it; thread 7 blue beads and pass the wire through the middle bead of the next 5 beads.

157

12 On the other wire thread 3 blue beads and pass the wire through the middle of the next 5 beads.

13 On the lower wire thread 4 blue beads; on the higher wire thread 3 blue beads, and cross through 4 beads and through the next 5 beads.

14 On one of the wires thread 10 blue beads, and pass the wire through the fourth of the 7 beads in No. 9 on the same side as the wire.

15 Turn, pass the same wire through 5 of the 10 beads, thread 1 white bead and pass the wire through the next 5 beads remaining.

16 Repeat No. 14 and No. 15 with the other wire.

17 On one of the wires thread 1 white and 9 blue beads; on the other wire thread 1 white bead and cross through the 9 blue beads.

18 On one of the wires thread 3 blue beads; turn, miss 1, pass the wire through 2 beads.

19 On the same wire thread 11 blue beads; turn, miss 1, pass the wire through 2 beads.

20 With the other wire repeat No. 18 and No. 19.

21 On one of the wires thread 5 blue beads; take the other wire and cross through them.

22 On one of the wires thread 1 white bead and pass the wire through 4 beads just above it on the side of the seat commencing from the back; bend the wire backwards and cut it off. Repeat with the other wire.

Round Table

1 On a strong wire thread 3 blue, 3 white and 2 blue beads, and cross through 1 bead.

2 On one of the wires thread 4 blue, 1 white and 6 blue beads, and pass the wire through 7 beads, commencing from the white bead.

3 On one of the wires thread 8 blue beads, and cross the same wire through the first bead. Repeat with the other wire.

4 On one of the wires thread 6 blue, 1 white and 1 blue bead; pass the wire through the second bead from the white one in No. 2, repeat with the other wire.

5 On one of the wires thread 5 blue, 3 white and 2 blue beads; cross the wire through the third blue bead. Repeat with the other wire.

6 On one of the wires thread 4 blue beads and pass the wire downwards through 7 beads, commencing from the white bead; on the other wire thread 2 blue beads, and pass the wire downwards through the third of the 4 blue beads; again thread 1 blue bead and pass the wire downwards through 7 beads, commencing from the white bead.

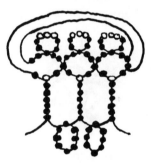

7 Thread 1 blue bead; take the other wire and cross through it.

8 On one of the wires thread 4 blue beads; on the other wire thread 3 blue beads, and cross through the fourth bead.

159

9 On the left wire thread 3 blue beads; take the other wire and cross through 1 bead.

10 (On one of the wires thread 2 blue beads; on the other wire thread 1 blue bead and cross through 1 bead. Five times.)

11 Pass the inner wire through the fourth of the next 7 beads, and thread 1 blue bead; on the other wire thread 1 blue bead and cross through 1 bead.

(On one of the wires thread 2 blue beads; on the other wire thread 1 blue bead and cross through 1 bead. Five times.)

12 Pass the inner wire through the fourth of the next 7 beads, and thread 1 blue bead; on the other wire thread 1 blue bead and cross through 1 bead.

13 (On one of the wires thread 2 blue beads; on the other wire thread 1 blue bead and cross through 1 bead. Four times.)

14 On the inner wire thread 1 blue bead, and pass the wire outwards through the first bead in No. 9, then thread 1 blue bead and with the other wire cross through it.

(On one of the wires thread 5 blue beads, and pass the wire through the second bead of the last round. Eight times.)

15 Thread 5 blue beads; twist both wires together and cut them off.

Bed

To make the mattress

1 On a strong wire 1¼ yards long thread 8 blue beads and cross through the first and second beads.

2 (On one of the wires thread 4 blue beads; on the other wire thread 2 blue beads and cross through 2 beads. Five times.)

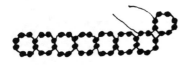

3 On one of the wires thread 6 blue beads; take the other wire and cross through 2 beads.

4 On the right hand wire thread 8 blue beads; take the other wire and cross through 2 beads.

5 On the same wire thread 4 blue beads; cross the other wire through 2 beads.

6 (Pass the inner wire through the 2 beads next to it, and thread 2 blue beads; on the other wire thread 2 blue beads, then cross through 2 beads. Six times.)

7 On the inner wire thread 6 blue beads; cross the other wire through 2 beads.

8 On the end wire thread 6 blue beads; cross the other wire through 2 beads.

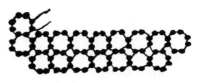

9 (Pass the inner wire through the 2 beads next to it, and thread 2 blue beads; on the other wire thread 2 blue beads, then cross through 2 beads. Seven times.)

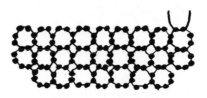

10 Pass the inner wire through the 2 beads next to it, and thread 4 blue beads; cross the inner wire through 2 beads.

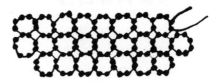

11 On the end wire thread 6 blue beads; cross the other wire through 2 beads.

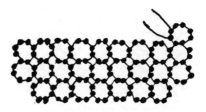

161

12 (Pass the inner wire through the 2 beads next to it, and thread 2 blue beads; on the other wire thread 2 blue beads, and cross through 2 beads. Seven times.)

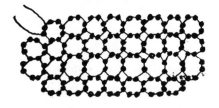

13 Pass the inner wire through the 2 beads next to it, and thread 4 blue beads; cross the other wire through 2 beads.

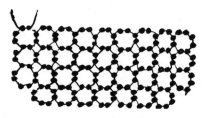

14 On the left hand wire thread 6 blue beads; cross the other wire through 2 beads.

15 (Pass the inner wire through the 2 beads next to it, and thread 2 blue beads; on the other wire thread 2 blue beads, then cross through 2 beads. Six times.)

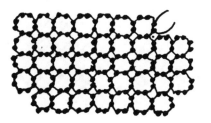

16 Pass the inner wire through the 2 beads next to it; pass the wire from right to left through the next 2 beads, and again through the second of the 6 beads.

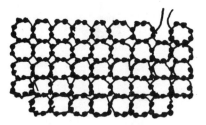

17 On one of the wires thread 2 blue beads; cross the other wire through the 2 beads.

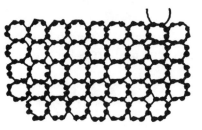

18 On the right hand wire thread 6 blue beads; cross the other wire through 2 beads.

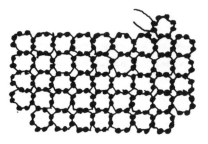

19 (Pass the inner wire through the 2 beads next to it and thread 2 blue beads; thread 2 blue beads on the other wire and cross through 2 beads. Five times.)

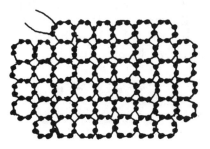

20 Pass the inner wire through the 2 beads next to it, and thread 4 blue beads; cross the other wire through 2 beads.

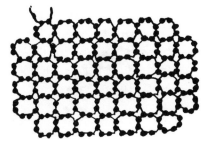

21 On the wire near the corner thread 4 blue beads; cross the other wire through 1 bead.

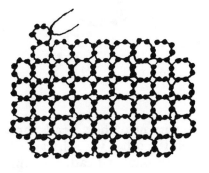

22 (Pass the inner wire through the 2 beads next to it, and thread 1 blue bead; on the other wire thread 2 blue beads and cross through 1 bead. Six times.)
On one of the wires thread 2 blue and 1 white bead; on the other wire thread 2 blue beads and cross through 1 bead; thread 3 blue beads; on the other wire thread 2 blue beads and cross through 1 bead.

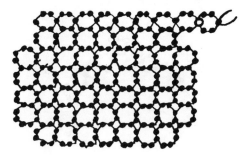

23 Pass the lower or inner wire through the fifth and sixth beads in No. 16, then thread 1 blue bead; on the other wire thread 2 blue beads, and cross through 1 bead.
Continue working as follows until the border is completed:

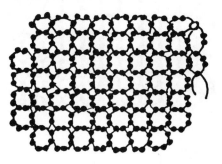

24 (Pass the inner wire through the 2 beads next to it, and thread 1 blue bead. On the other wire thread 2 blue beads, and cross through 1 bead. Three times.)

25 On one of the wires thread 2 blue and 1 white bead; on the other wire thread 2 blue beads and cross through 1 bead; thread 3 blue beads; on the other wire thread 2 blue beads and cross through 1 bead.

26 Pass the inner wire through the 2 beads round the corner, then thread 1 blue bead; on the other wire thread 2 blue beads and cross through 1 bead.

27 (Pass the inner wire through the 2 beads next to it, and thread 1 blue bead; thread 2 blue beads on the other wire and cross through 1 bead. Six times.)

28 On one of the wires thread 2 blue and 1 white bead; on the other wire thread 2 blue beads and cross through 1 bead; thread 3 blue beads; on the other wire thread 2 blue beads, and cross through 1 bead.

29 Pass the inner wire through the fifth and sixth beads in No. 16 then thread 1 blue bead; on the other wire thread 2 blue beads and cross through 1 bead.

30 (Pass the inner wire through the 2 beads next to it, and thread 1 blue bead; on the other wire thread 2 blue beads, then cross through 1 bead. Three times.)

31 On one of the wires thread 2 blue and 1 white bead; on the other wire thread 2 blue beads, and cross through 1 bead.

32 On the inner wire thread 2 blue beads and pass the wire outwards through the first of the 4 beads in No. 21.

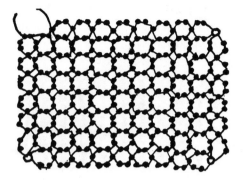

33 On one of the wires thread 2 blue beads; twist both wires together and cut them off. This completes the mattress.

To make the canopy

34 On a wire ¾ yard long thread 6 blue beads and cross through the first bead.

35 On one of the wires thread 3 blue beads; on the other wire thread 1 blue bead, and cross through 1 bead.

36 (On the wire near the 2 beads thread 3 blue beads; on the other wire thread 1 blue bead, and cross through 1 bead. Four times.)

37 On the wire near the 2 beads thread 7 white beads, and cross through the first and second beads. (Note the first and second beads must be large enough for 3 wires to go through them.)

38 On the wire near the blue beads thread 2 blue beads; cross the other wire through 1 bead.

39 (On the wire near the 2 beads thread 3 blue beads; on the other wire thread 1 blue bead and cross through 1 bead. Five times.)

40 On the wire near the 2 beads thread 4 blue beads; on the other wire thread 1 blue bead, and cross through 1 bead.

41 (On one of the wires thread 2 blue beads; on the other wire thread 1 blue bead, and cross through 1 bead. Six times.)

42 On the inner wire thread 1 blue bead and pass the wire downwards through the third bead in No. 34, then thread 1 blue bead; cross the other wire through 1 bead.

43 On the right hand wire thread 3 blue beads; cross the other wire through 1 bead.

44 (Pass the inner wire through the bead next to it, and thread 1 blue bead; on the other wire thread 1 blue bead, then cross through 1 bead. Six times.)

45 Pass the inner wire through the bead next to it, and thread 1 white bead; on the other wire thread 1 blue bead, then cross through the white bead.

46 (Pass the inner wire through the 2 beads next to it, and thread 1 blue bead; on the other wire thread 2 blue beads, and cross through 1 bead. Twelve times.)

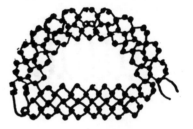

47 Pass the inner wire through the 2 beads next to it, and thread 1 white bead; on the other wire thread 2 blue beads, and cross through the white bead.

48 Pass the inner wire through the 2 single beads next to it, and thread 1 blue bead; twist both wires together and cut off.

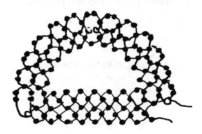

To make the bed head

49 On a wire 1 yard long thread 21 blue beads, and cross through 7 beads.

50 (On one of the wires thread 8 blue beads; on the other wire thread 1 blue bead, and cross through 7 beads. Six times.)

51 On the higher wire thread 4 blue beads; on the other wire thread 10 blue beads, and cross through 2 beads.

52 On the right hand or inner wire thread 13 blue beads; miss the 6 single beads and the next 2, then pass the wire through 2 beads.

To attach the canopy to the bed head

53 On one of the wires thread 10 blue beads; pass the wire through the 2 beads next to the white bead on the side of the canopy; thread 1 blue bead and pass the wire through the next 2 beads; thread 8 blue beads, miss 4 of the 10 beads, counting from the white bead and pass the wire through the remaining 6 beads. Repeat with the other wire.

To attach the canopy and bed head to the mattress

54 On the left hand wire thread 15 blue beads; join to the mattress by passing the wire through the third and fourth beads from the white bead.

55 Thread 1 blue bead; pass the wire through the next 2 beads; thread 4 blue beads, pass the wire upwards through 11 beads, from the eleventh to the first of the 15 beads, then downwards through the 9 beads next to it. Repeat with the other wire.

56 On one of the wires thread 3 blue beads, and pass the wire downwards through the white bead next to it. Repeat with the other wire.

To make the legs

57 On one of the wires thread 5 blue and 1 white bead; turn, miss 1 bead, pass the wire upwards through the 5 beads and through the next 2 beads on the side of the mattress. Draw tight and cut wire off.

58 Repeat from No. 54 with the other wire.

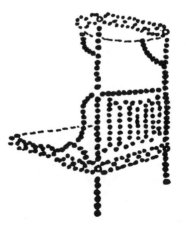

To make the bed end

59 On another wire thread 13 blue beads; cross through the first, second and third beads.

60 (On one of the wires thread 4 blue beads; on the other wire thread 1 blue bead, and cross through 3 beads. Six times.)

61 On the lower wire thread 8 blue beads. On the other wire thread 2 blue beads, then cross through 2 beads.

62 On the inner wire thread 13 blue beads; miss the 6 single beads and the next 2, then pass the wire through 2 beads.

63 On one of the wires thread 2 white beads; turn, miss 1 bead, and pass the next 5 blue beads; then thread 2 blue beads, pass the wire downwards through the white bead on the mattress; again thread 5 blue beads and 1 white one; turn, miss the white bead, and pass the wire upwards through the 5 blue beads, then through the next 2 beads on the side of the mattress. Cut the wire off. Repeat with the other wire.

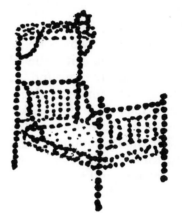

The origin of the foregoing patterns

IN the course of collecting material for this book, one incident has intrigued me above all others. It concerns a certain Miss Smith who published in 1889 what is, as far as I can discover, the first book on beadwork. It was called *Bead Furniture and Ornamental Beadwork*. It consists of two parts, each little more than a leaflet, on making bead furniture for a doll's house. There were to be thirty-six parts and the price was sixpence.

Curious to find out what happened to the other thirty-four parts, I looked up the entry in the register of the Stationers' Hall, and learnt that her name was Margaret and that she lived at 764 Scotswood Road, Newcastle upon Tyne.

Still not satisfied, I tried the Voters' Register and discovered there that her name was not Margaret but Mary, and that in 1895 she changed the number of her house to 756. A year later she had gone without trace. As her name does not appear in the register of Births, Marriages and Deaths, we can only assume that she moved away from the city to an unknown destination, leaving her book to haunt an obscure corner of a great library. It is one of those sad stories the end of which we shall never be told.

Her diagrams have been re-drawn, but the instructions and lay-out are substantially as she arranged them.

Part VII Beadweaving

Bead weaving on a bow loom

MAN, in the first years of his existence, learnt to construct wind-breaks, which he badly needed in his constant battle with the elements, by driving stakes into the ground and winding boughs and vines amongst them. Later he adapted this technique for making mats of rushes, grass or bark, and so gradually the way was paved for the invention of the loom.

Like all primitive tools it was extremely simple but quite effective, and was probably invented many times over in different areas and at different periods of time. Somebody took a branch, bent it between his hands like a bow or a water diviner's rod, and tied the ends together with a series of strings. As the branch struggled to regain its natural position, it pulled the strings taut and held them there, and so it became apparent that by working a few twigs in and out of them at either end of the bow, or by passing them round a cross-piece lashed at right angles to it, they would remain not only tight but also evenly spaced, and a rough and ready warp had been achieved.

This bow loom, like the bow drill, is still in use in various parts of the world. The example illustrated was collected not long ago in the interior of New Guinea and illustrates the most primitive method of bead weaving.

In setting up the warp it is essential that there is always one more warp thread than there are beads in the pattern.

If the bow is held between the knees, the string on which the beads for the first row are threaded, should be attached to the end of the loom, and also to the first warp thread on the left hand side. It is then passed *under* the warp from left to right, and as it goes the beads are pushed up from below by the left hand, and so arranged that a warp thread lies on each side of every bead. The thread is then tightened; the needle taken *above* the warp, and passed *through* the beads from right to left. In other words, the beads which were placed below the warp on the first journey, were secured above the warp on the return (211).

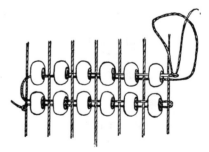

211 Simple beadweaving technique showing the needle which has carried the weft thread from left to right below the warp, on its return journey through the beads.
'Beads and Beadwork of the American Indians',
William C. Orchard

When the thread is finished or breaks, it can be repaired with a weaver's knot. A broken warp thread is repaired in the same way (212).

If a pattern is being followed each row of beads has to be threaded with great care as one mistake can create utter nonsense out of the easiest design.

But the natives of British Guiana and parts of the Amazon region, use the bow loom in a totally different fashion. Their loom consists of a more deeply curved bow with a cross-piece of wood fixed to its extremities, which serves not only to keep the loom in position, but also as a beam from which the warp threads are suspended. With it they weave small, beaded aprons, shaped with considerable ingenuity, and worked in a variety of patterns. They are woven upside-down, and from right to left.

The woman—and weaving in the Guianas is always done by the women—begins by fastening four strings across the bow, about mid-way between the cross-piece and the base, leaving long ends on either side which eventually become the tie strings for the completed apron. The warp threads are woven into these four threads as shown in the diagram, and when they are pulled tight, they form the upper selvedge edge of the apron. They are separated into groups of about six strands and tied loosely to the cross-piece.

The woman squats on the ground, or sits in easy comfort in a hammock, and thrusts her legs through the bow. She doubles a thread round the first warp thread on her right hand side and proceeds to string beads on this double thread. The first row at least is worked only in one colour. She unties the first group of threads, and passes each strand in its proper order, through the doubled string of beads, so that one warp thread comes between two beads. When this is finished, the group of warp threads is tied once again to the cross-piece and the next group treated in the same way.

At the end of each row the warp threads are twisted around so that they will hold the weft in place as it is pushed down on to the row below. The loom is then turned round ensuring that the beading proceeds from right to left.

When she wishes to increase the width of the apron, the woman ties in an extra pair of warp threads. A supply of spare threads specially for this purpose is usually kept tied in readiness on

212 *Weaver's knot*

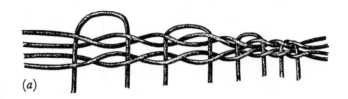

(a)

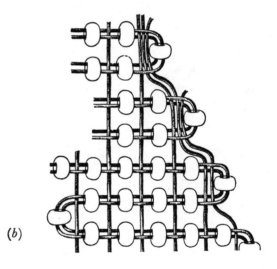

(b)

213 *Diagrams showing*
(a) *the arrangement of the warp threads on the upper edge of a beaded apron*
(b) *the way in which the sides of the apron are shaped by reducing the number of warp threads as the work proceeds*
'*Beads and Beadwork of the American Indians*',
William C. Orchard

169

one side of the bow. When the weaving is completed the warp ends are beaded so that they form a fringe.

The patterns are usually geometric but they also weave a very attractive design of monkeys, and this can be studied on an apron in the Pitt Rivers Museum, Oxford, which was collected as recently as 1954. It is possible to distinguish several species of monkey among those represented. The colours are chiefly blue, white, and pink.

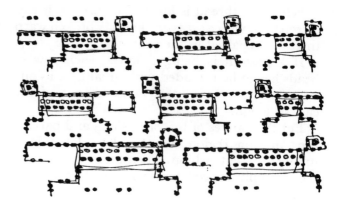

214 Monkeys woven in a beaded apron: British Guiana
Pitt Rivers Museum, Oxford

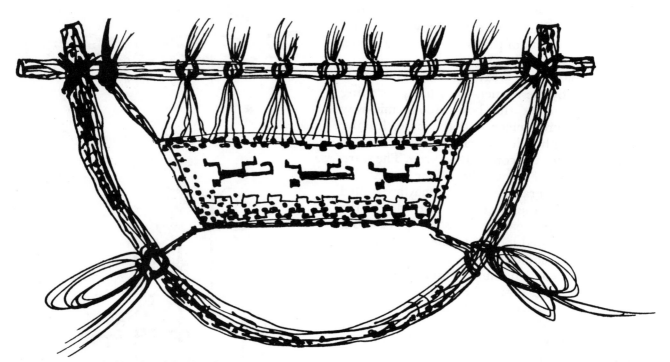

215 Bow loom with strip of beadwork in progress: New Guinea   *British Museum*

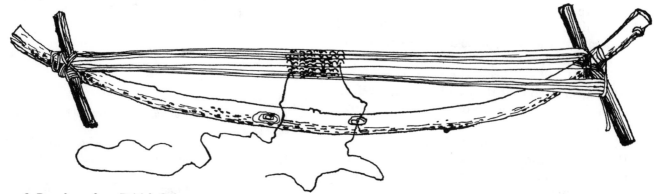

216 Bow loom from British Guiana
Pitt Rivers Museum, Oxford

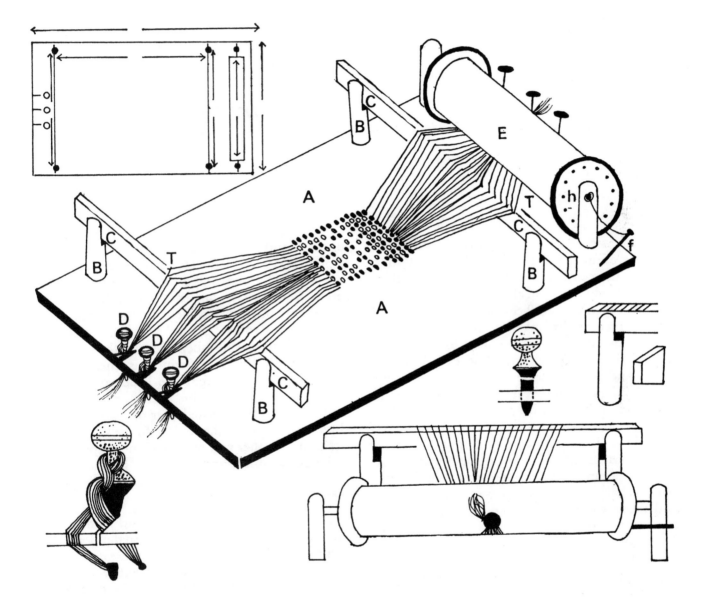

217 Austin's bead loom of 1903. Note that the frets carrying the warp threads slope towards the centre of the board

IT has sometimes been said that beads were loom woven in the late eighteenth century, but I have found no reliable evidence to support this, rather the contrary; and although a search of the records in the Patent Office revealed a number of curious recipes for making beads, a permit granted in 1631 to Sir William Bruckner for 'making kersie seeves, otherwise called twillie seeves, and bedes of bone and wood', and some extraordinary machines for threading beads, it produced no bead looms prior to 1903. In that year, however, Herbert Aurelius Austin, described as a manufacturer, of 109 Kingston Street, Boston, Mass., applied for a patent for 'a loom frame for weaving beadwork belts, sashes, chains, fob chains, purses, and bags, the said frame comprising simple means of holding the warp threads any desired distance apart from each other, for clamping the ends of said threads, and for winding up the finished work'. Patent No. 17617 was granted to him on 29th October in the same year. It was called 'The Apache Loom'. In all probability the American patent was taken out a few months previously (217).

The loom, Austin wrote, is constructed with a base (A), fitted with uprights (B), carrying two notched frets (C), over which the warp threads (T) are laid. The warp threads are secured at one end to pegs (D), and the other ends are tied together and secured to a roller (E), which is then rotated to produce the necessary tension, and locked by inserting a pin (f) in one of the series of holes (h) in one end. The weft thread is tied to an outer warp close to the comb (C), nearest to the roller (E), and a number of beads, one less than the number of warp threads, are threaded on the weft, which is then passed below the warps so that the beads project up between the warps. The needle carrying the weft thread is then passed over the warps, being threaded through the beads to lock them in position. Another row of beads is next applied in a similar manner; and so on, the finished work being wound up on the roller (E) in making long webs.

It is clear then that various bead looms were on sale in both America and England at the beginning of this century, but there were also others of simpler construction, that were easily made at home. Mary White tells us that more than one weaver has done excellent work on a loom made out of an empty cigar box, and proceeds to give these instructions for making one:

The sides are cut down within an inch of the bottom, and a small piece of wood, the depth of the box, is fastened inside each corner to support the end pieces. Small notches one eighth of an inch apart are cut along the ends of these to hold the warp threads in place. Six tacks are driven in below the notches on the outside ends at equal distances apart. Upon these the ends of the warp are wound (219).

In place of the comb some people may find it easier to thread a number of beads on two wires which are then laid across the blocks to carry the warp. This is not a bad idea as it allows the space between the warp threads to match the beads on the weft exactly. The practical little loom or beading frame shown (220) turned up recently in a London street market stall and also dates from the same period.

Many long watch and fob chains were made on these looms by the method described in the preceding chapter. The ends can be joined together, (i) by fastening them to a metal clasp; (ii) by securing them to a piece of chamois leather which was the method usually chosen by Indian weavers; and (iii) by making an additional piece of weaving in the form of a plaque or end piece. To do this, bring the warp threads at either end together, and fasten them to the loom in a single row. On this double-sized warp weave a solid square, threading one more bead than is necessary, and placing it between the two inner warp threads so that both sides are joined together. Finally, beads of the same size and colour as the chain are strung on the ends of the warp threads to make a fringe; the ends of the threads being run back through each strand, starting at the next bead but one to the end, and finishing by sewing each to the edge of the woven square.

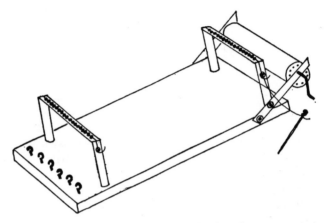

218 Roller type loom in which the warp threads are separated by beads. This is the loom recommended by Mary White in 'How to do beadwork'

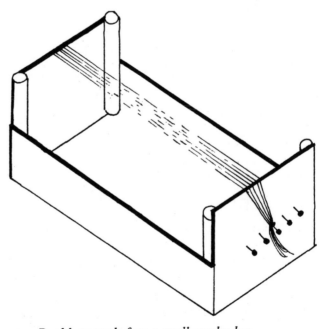

219 Bead loom made from a small wooden box

173

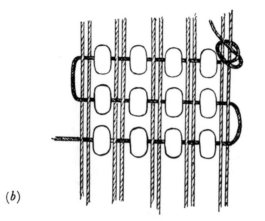

(b)

(b) Technique of weaving with a double thread for the weft

221 A form of weaving called Bead Mosaic was made between two perforated cards through which the warp was carried. One end was knotted and attached to a heavy cushion and the other was often attached to the weaver's belt

220(a) Bead weaving frame 7″ × 14″ made from four round poles held together at the corners by pegs. The two shorter poles are grooved and the warp thread is wound continuously around the frame from end to end; this produces a double warp which is useful if heavy beads are to be woven

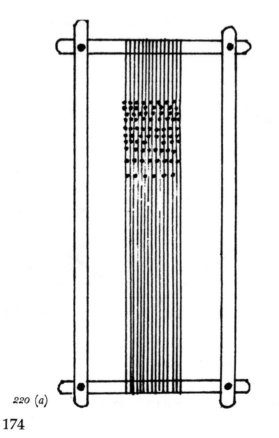

220 (a)

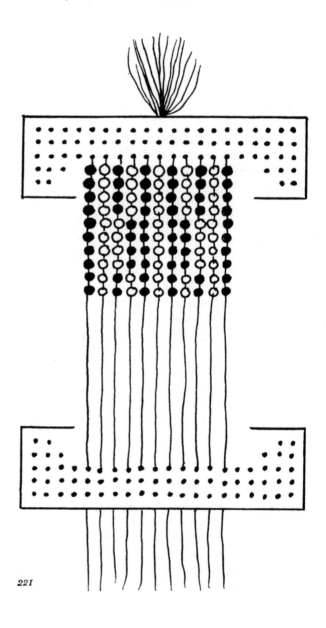

221

174

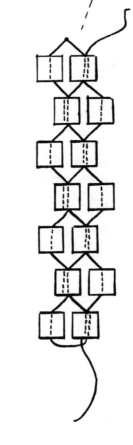

222 *Beaded mat, showing extension and reduction in weaving*

223 *Diagram showing how simple bead weaving with needle and thread is extended*

Weaving with needle and thread

WITHOUT even the simplest loom and with no specially prepared warp, beads can be woven in the hand with needle and thread. This is a very ancient form of beadwork and produces a texture like brickwork, each bead fitting into the little gap between two beads in the preceding row, rather than lying directly one above the other as in loomed work.

Take two needlefuls of thread double the length of trimming required. Double the thread in half and knot all four ends together. Should the thread be very strong it can be used singly. Pin the ends firmly down to a leaded pincushion. Thread one bead on the right hand strand, and pass the left needle through it backwards, so that its tip points towards the cushion. Take the left needle in the right hand and the right needle in the left hand, and draw both threads through a bead, pushing it as far as it will go towards the knot end of the threads. Thread two beads on the right needle and one on the left. Pass the left hand strand through the second bead of the right hand one, and draw the three beads evenly up to the end. This forms a sort of diamond shaped pattern. Again pass two beads on to the right hand strand and one on the left; cross the left hand strand through the second bead so that it becomes the right hand strand. Continue working in this way until the trimming is long enough. Fasten off tightly by knotting the ends of the thread close to the last bead.

The pattern is made wider by joining in another row, made in a similar manner to the first, but using two beads instead of three. Leave the first part of the trimming attached to the cushion, prepare two needlefuls of thread as before, and tie the ends together, pinning them to the cushion beside the first part of the trimming. Pass one bead on to the right hand strand and cross the left hand strand through it. Thread two beads on the right hand strand, pass the left hand needle through the first side bead of the right hand side of the piece of trimming, then through the second bead on the right hand strand. Draw the beads up as before. Thread two beads on the right hand strand, pass the left needle through the next side bead of the trimming, then through the second bead on the right hand strand, and continue thus until the second piece is as long as the first.

Choose beads of regular size so that the various sets of beads rest freely and evenly against each other, but yet are not so near as to fret and break the threads, or to look loose and slovenly when the trimming is in use.

Another method was used to make the beaded mats that came into fashion about 1858. What a writer described as 'one of the prettiest mats which has yet been invented', was made—

rather alarmingly—of crystal beads strung on pink crochet cotton, which, we are told, 'produced such changeableness of hue as to give it the most elegant appearance'. 'To make this mat', she goes on, 'take double crochet cotton and as many beads as will measure across the size required; then return, taking up a bead on the needle, and one on the string, alternately, until the end going backwards and forwards in the same way until the whole is completed. We recommend this mat for its tasteful appearance, which must be seen to be appreciated'.

Fig. 224 shows how beads of two different sizes can be woven into vandykes with needle and thread. Necklaces can be made in this way or by the methods illustrated in fig. 226. Fig. 227 shows one of the ways in which the Indians of North America introduced colours into their needle weaving.

225 Diagram of diagonal weaving

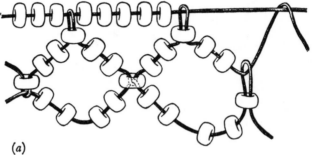

(a)

(b)

(c)

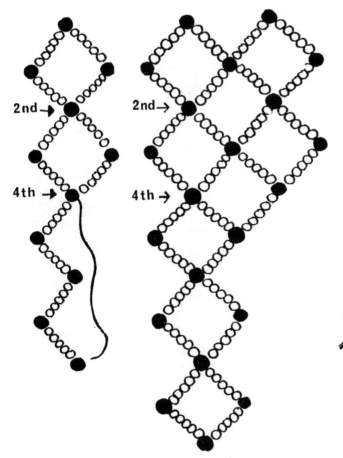

224 This method of weaving a diamond-shaped mesh is useful for making bags and is also the technique employed in making vandyked trimmings or necklaces

226 (a) (b) (c) Three different techniques developed by the American Indians for weaving a beaded mesh for bags or necklaces

177

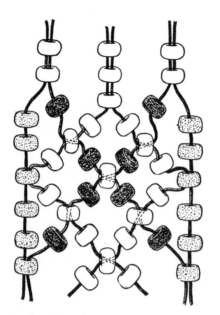

227 Detail of necklace from Ecuador
'Beads and Beadwork of the American Indians',
William C. Orchard

228

228–9 Figures from beaded chains. By using an equal number
of warp strands and beads a picot edge is obtained which was
often used effectively on these chains

Victoria and Albert Museum

Bibliography

Part I

The First Bead Embroidery

'Beadworkers of Ilorin, Nigeria', *Man*, 2. Daniel, F. London 1937.

The Stone Age on Mount Carmel. Garrod, D. A. E. London 1937.

Woman's Share in Primitive Culture. Mason, O. T. London 1894.

'Beadmaking with a Bow Drill on the Gold Coast', *Journal of the Royal Anthropological Institute*, LXXV. Shaw, E. T. London 1945.

Leaflet No. 30. Denver Art Museum. Department of Indian Art. 1931.

Shell Beads

Argonauts of the Western Pacific. Malinowski, B. London 1922.

Beads and Beadwork of the American Indians. Orchard, W. C. London 1929.

Origin of the Word Bead

A Bibliography of Folklore. Bonser, W. London 1962.

'Beads and Knots', *Folklore*, 25. Gaster, M. London 1914.

A Dictionary of London. Harben, H. London 1918.

'Folklore in London', *Folklore.* Lovett, A. E. London 1913.

'The Folklore of Children's Diseases', *Folklore*, 54. Rolleston, J. D. London 1943.

Memorials of London and London Life in the XIII, XIV, and XV centuries. Riley, T. H. London 1868.

Notes and Queries, Second Series, III. London 1857.

Bugles

An Historical and Chronological Deduction of the Origin of Commerce, IV. Anderson, A. London 1787.

'Beadmaking at Murano, Venice', *Journal of the Royal Society of Arts.* London 1919.

Glass. Dillon, E. London 1907.

General Dictionary of Trade and Commerce. Mortimer, T. London 1810.

Annals of St Olave's, Hart Street. Povah, A. London 1894.

The History of the Hudson's Bay Company. Rich, E. E. London 1958.

'Ancient Glass Beads', *Journal of the Royal Anthropological Institute*, LXXXVIII. Van Der Sleen, W. London 1959 and *Man*, 219, London 1963.

Elegant Arts for Ladies. London 1854.

Lady's Book, XLIX. Godey's. Philadelphia, Pa. 1854, 1855.

Trade Beads in East Africa

First Footsteps in East Africa. Burton, Sir R. F. London 1856.

The Lake Regions of Central Africa. Burton, Sir R. F. London 1860.

Zanzibar; City, Island and Coast. Burton, Sir R. F. London 1872.

'Nineteenth Century Trade Beads in Tanganyika', *Man.* Harding, J. R. London, July 1962.

Catalogue of an Exhibition. Staub, P. Rhodes National Gallery, Salisbury, Rhodesia, June/July 1961.

How I Found Livingstone. Stanley, H. M. London 1872.

Zambesi Expedition of David Livingstone. Wallis, J. P. R. London 1956.

Stuart Beadwork

The Tatler, 247. Steele, R. London 1710.

'English Needlework in the Lady Lever Art Gallery', *Apollo.* Tait, A. C. London, May and July 1947.

Domestic Needlework. Seligman, G. S. and Hughes, T. London 1962.

The Art of Embroidery. Schuette, M. and Müller-Christensen, S. London 1964.

Lace Bugle

The Progresses and Public Processions of Queen Elizabeth, III. Nichols, J.

History of Lace. Palliser, F. B. London 1865.

Royal and Historic Gloves and Shoes. Redfern, W. B. London 1904.

The Shepheardes Calender. Spenser, E. London 1579.

Buglework

'English Domestic Embroidery Patterns of the XVI and XVII centuries', Walpole Society, XXVIII. Nevison, J. L. London 1940.

Spangles, Sequins and Artificial Jewels

Costume in the Drama of Shakespeare and his Contemporaries. Linthicum, M. C. Oxford 1936.

The History of Sir Charles Grandison. Richardson, S. London 1753.

L'art du brodeur. Saint-Aubin, C. G. de. Paris 1770.

Englishwoman's Domestic Magazine. London 1866.

Lady's Book, XXVII. Godey's. Philadelphia, Pa. 1843.

The Lady's Magazine. London 1801.

On Buying Beads

Ancient Inventories. Halliwell, J. O. London 1854.

A Dictionary of Archaic and Provincial Words. Halliwell, J. O. London 1865.

The Ladies' Handbook. Hartley, F. London 1859.

Victorian Embroidery. Morris, B. London 1962.

Household Books of Lord William Howard of Naworth. Surtees Society, VXVIII. London 1878.

Pearl Embroidery

British Freshwater Bivalve Molluscs. Ellis, A. E. London 1962.

La broderie du XIe siècle jusqu'à nos jours. Farcy, L. de. Paris 1890.

Glossaire archaeologique du Moyen Age et de la Renaissance. Gay, V. Paris 1928.

Shells as Evidence of the Migrations of Early Cultures. Jackson, J. W. London 1917.

'Notes on Irish Pearls'. *Irish Naturalists' Journal*, IX. Went, A. E. J.

Russian Pearl Embroidery

The Kremlin. Duncan, D. D. London 1960.

Russkoe shit'e zhemchugom. Yakunina, L. I. Moscow 1955.

Artificial Pearls

The Art of Glass. Blancourt, H. de. London 1669.

The Technical Repository, 7. Gill, T. London 1825.

Sloane MSS. No. 857. London.

Lady's Book, XIX. Godey's. Philadelphia, Pa. 1838.

Crystals and Jet

The Gem Cutter's Craft. Claremont, L. London 1906.

Glass. Dillon, E. London 1907.

A History of Jewellery, 1100–1870. Evans, Joan. London 1953.

Some Small Jet Carvings Produced at Santiago de Compostela. Hildburgh, W. L. London 1917.

Letter Books of Sir Amias Poulet. Morris, J. London 1874.

Memorials of London and London Life in the XIII, XIV, and XV centuries. Riley, T. London 1868.

'The Rosary', *The Month*, XCVI and XCVII. Thurston, H., S. J. London 1900 and 1901.

Englishwoman's Domestic Magazine. London 1861, 1862, 1867.

Lady's Book, LVI. Godey's. Philadelphia, Pa. 1858.

Coral Embroidery

Introduction to the Study of Recent Corals. Hickson, S. J. London 1924.

Histoire naturelle du corail. Lacaze-Duthiers, J. Paris 1864.

'A Brief Sketch of the Red or Precious Coral', *The Zoologist*. McIntosh, W. C. London, January 1910.

La pêche et la fabrication du corail. Mégy, Barbaroux de. Paris 1844.

'Precious Coral', *Nature*. Moseley, H. N. London 1882 and 1885.

The Amateur's Art Designer. London, July 1890.

The Manufacture of Embroidery Beads

'Journal of a Tour of the Coast of the Adriatic Sea', *Edinburgh Philosophical Journal*, XVI. Hoppe, D. H. and Hornschurch, H. London.

The Worshipful Company of Glass-Sellers of London. Howard, A. L. London 1940.

Glassmacherkunst. Kunckel, J. von Lowenstein. Nürnberg 1756.

The Arts of Glass. Neri, A. Florence 1612.

Glass Making in England. Powell, H. J. London 1923.

English Industries of the Middle Ages. Salzmann, L. F. London 1913.

Five Thousand Years of Glassmaking. Vavra, J. R. Prague 1954.

History of the Worshipful Company of Glass-Sellers of London. Young, S. London 1913.

'Beadmaking at Murano and Venice'. A consular report. *Journal of the Royal Society of Arts.* London, August 1919.

A Home Industry

Gli abiti de Veneziani di quasi ogni eta con diligenza raccolti e dipinzi nel secolo XVIII. MSS. III. Greuenbroch, J. Correr Library, Venice.

Bead making in America

'Barcelona Glass in Venetian Style', *Hispanic Society of America*. Frothingham, A. W. New York 1956.

Glassmaking at Jamestown, America's First Industry. Harrington, J. C. London 1952.

The Roanoke Voyages 1548–1590. Quinn, D. B. Hakluyt Society. London 1955.

Beadwork of the American Indians

Beads and Beadwork of the American Indians. Orchard, W. C. London 1929.

'Moccasins and their Quillwork', *Journal of the Royal Anthropological Institute*, XXXVIII. Roth, H. Ling. London 1908.

'Hair Embroidery in Siberia and North America', *Pitt Rivers Occasional Papers on Technology*, No. 7. Turner, G. Oxford.

Crow Indian Beadwork. Wildschut, W. and Ewers, J. C. London 1959.

Wampum

History and Present State of Virginia. Beverley, R. 1705. Other editions 1722, 1855 and 1947.

Art of the North West Coast Indians. Inverarity, R. B. London 1950.

The History of the Mission of the United Brethren among the Indians of North America. Loskiel, G. H. London 1794.

Beads and Beadwork of the American Indians. Orchard, W. C. London 1925.

The Penn Wampum Belts. Orchard, W. C. London 1925.

A Key to the Language of America. Williams, R. London 1643.

Leaflets Nos. 31 (1931), 59 and 60 (1933), and 112 (1951). Denver Art Museum, Department of Indian Art.

Zulu Talking Beads

Zulu Beadwork: The Language of Colours. Mayr, Rev. Father F. Annals of the Pietermaritzburg Museum, Natal. Part 2, 1907.

Part II

Beading by Machine

La broderie mécanique, 1828–1930. Iklé, E. Paris 1931.

Les pionniers de la technique de la broderie mécanique. Rust, E. Zurich 1920.

Tambour Beading

Encyclopedia of Needlework. Dillmont, T. de. Alsace 1897.

The Beaders

Money-making for Ladies. Church, E. R. New York 1882.

Needlework for Ladies. Dorinda. London 1883.

Cranford. Gaskell, Mrs E. C. London 1853.

'Home Work in Berlin', *Economics Journal*, VIII. Veen, M. van der. London 1898.

The Amateur's Art Designer. London, July 1891.

The Handbook of the Daily News Sweated Industries Exhibition. London 1906.

Home Industries of Women in London. Report of the Women's Industrial Council. London 1906.

Passementerie

'Working Women in Vienna', *Economics Journal*, VII. Levetus, A. S. London 1897.

La pratique de l'aiguille industrieuse. Migerak, M. Paris 1605.

The Lady's Magazine. London, March 1891.

Parts III to VII

General

The Dictionary of Needlework. Caulfeild and Saward. London 1892.

Englishwoman's Domestic Magazine. London.

Sy og voev med perler. Erlandsen, I. M. Copenhagen 1957.

Lady's Book. Godey's. Philadelphia, Pa.

Beadcraft. Littlejohns, I. B. London 1929.

The Illuminated Ladies' Book of Useful and Ornamental Needlework. Owen, Mrs Henry. London 1847.

The Priscilla Beadwork Book. Robinson, B. Boston, Mass. 1912.

Bead Furniture and Ornamental Beadwork. Smith, M. Parts I and II. Newcastle upon Tyne 1889.

Practical Needlework series. Weldon's. London c. 1900.

How to do Beadwork. White, M. New York 1904.

Glasperlen und Perlen-arbeiten in alter und neuer zeit. Pazaurek, G. E. Darmstadt 1911.

The following additional sources have become available since the original edition of this book:

The Bead Emboidered Dress. Edwards, Joan. 1985

Beadwork. Clabburn, Pamela. Shire 1980

Beads and Beadwork of East and South Africa. Margaret Carey. Shire 1986

Beads and Beadwork of West and Central Africa. Margaret Carey. Shire 1991

The Book of Beads. Coles, Janet and Budwig, Robert. Simon & Schuster 1990

Des Dorelotiers Aux Passementiers. Gasc, Nadine. Musée des Arts Décoratifs 1973

Hautè Couture Embroidery: The Art of Lesage. White, Palmer. Vendome 1988

The History of Beads. Dubin, Lois Sherr. Abrams 1987

How To Bead, French Embroidery Beading. Jarratt, Maisie. Kangaroo 1991

Tambour Work. Fukuyama, Yusai. Dryad 1987

Those Bad Bad Beads. Virginia Blakelock 1988

Index

Numerals in *italics* refer to figure numbers

Sources

GREAT BRITAIN

BEAD SOCIETY OF GREAT BRITAIN
Formed in 1989 it is open to all interested in any aspect of bead work from a private or professional perspective. They hold 5 meeting a year, offering lectures, holding workshops and organizing a bead bazaar. The society publishes 5 newsletters a year.

> Carole Morris, Secretary
> THE BEAD SOCIETY OF GREAT BRITAIN
> 1 Casburn Lane
> Burwell, Cambridge
> ENGLAND   CB5 0ED

UNITED STATES

There are numerous independent Bead Societies covering virtually every region. A complete list of these (updated annually), as well as a listing of shops, museums and bazaars are listed in THE BEAD DIRECTORY:

> THE BEAD DIRECTORY
> Att: Linda Benmour
> PO Box 10103
> Oakland, CA 94610

Suppliers

GREAT BRITAIN

SPANGLES
Att: Carole Morris
1 Casburn Lane
Burwell, Cambridge
ENGLAND CB5 0ED

Retail and mail order.

ELLS AND FARRIER
THE BEAD HOUSE
Princess Street
London W.1.

BEADSHOP
43 Neal Street
London
ENGLAND WC2H 9PJ

Retail and mail order.

CREATIVE BEADCRAFT
Denmark Works
Sheepcote Dell Road
Beamad End
Nr Amersham
Bucks
ENGLAND HP7 0RX

Mail order only.

JANET COLES BEADS LTD.
Perdiswell Cottage
Bilford Road
Worcester
ENGLAND WR3 8QA

Mail order beads.

UNITED STATES

UNIVERSAL SYNERGETICS
16510 SW Edminston Rd.
Wilsonville, OR 97070-9514

Run by Virginia Blakelock and Carole Perrenoud, expert beaders. Specialty is high quality beads, vintage seed beads and innovative supplies. Mail order only. Catalog: $2.50

LACIS
2982 Adeline Street
Berkeley, CA 94703

Retail and mail order. Specialty is books and tools for beading, tambour and bead embroidery.

ORB WEAVER
4793 Telegraph Avenue
Oakland, CA 94609

Retail and mail order. Wide selection of beads. Classes offered.

ORNAMENTAL RESOURCES
1427 Miner Street
Idaho Springs, CO 80452

Extensive catalog, wide selection of beads.

SHIPWRECK BEADS, INC.
5021 Mud Bay Road
Olympia, WA 98502

Wholesale and retail and distributor prices. 65pg catalog

Author's Sketch Book Studies
(the following line drawings appeared in the original edition)

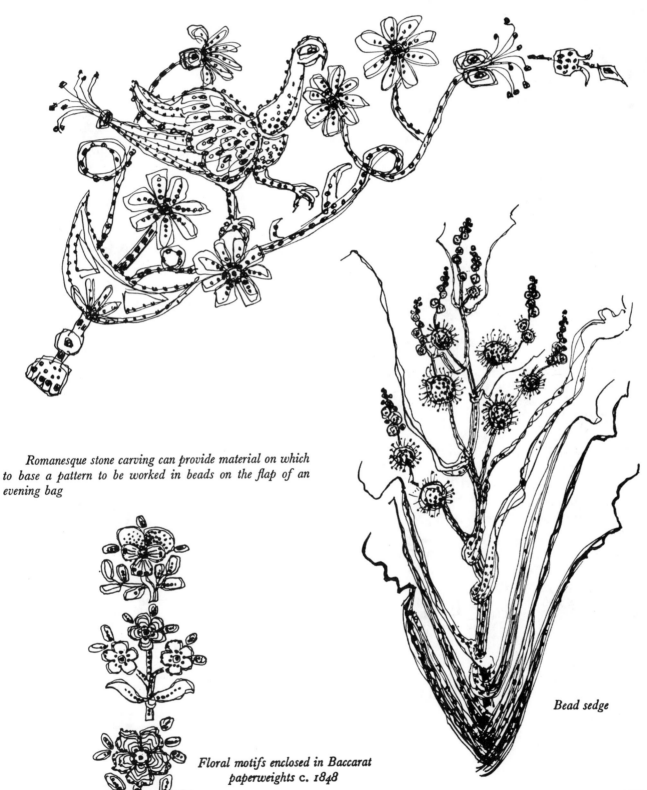

Romanesque stone carving can provide material on which to base a pattern to be worked in beads on the flap of an evening bag

Floral motifs enclosed in Baccarat paperweights c. 1848

Bead sedge

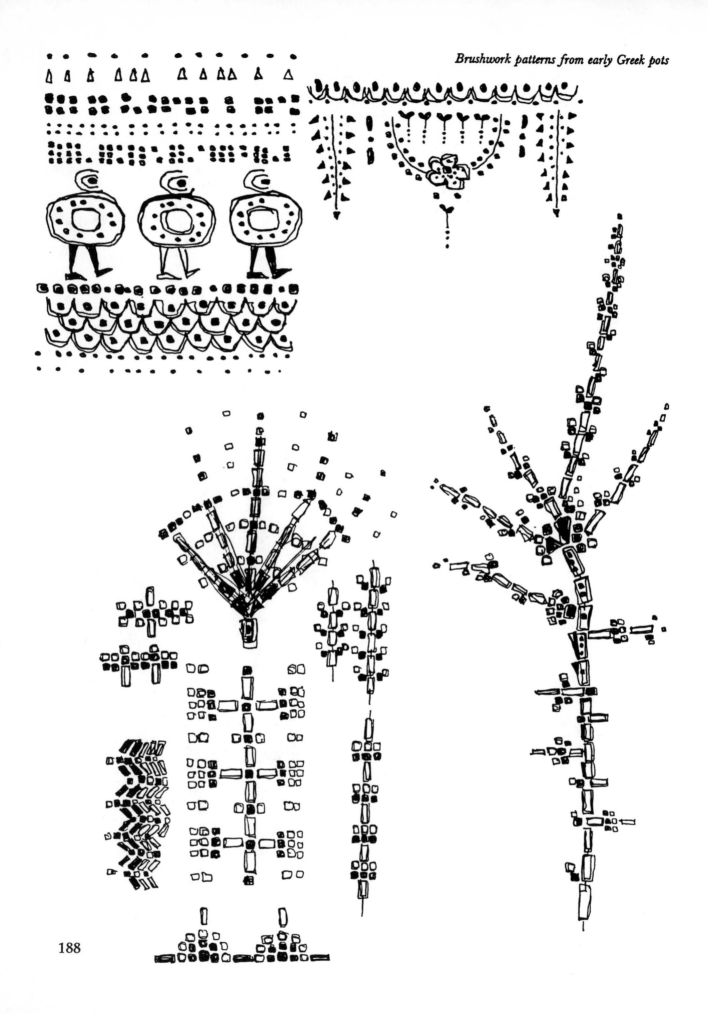

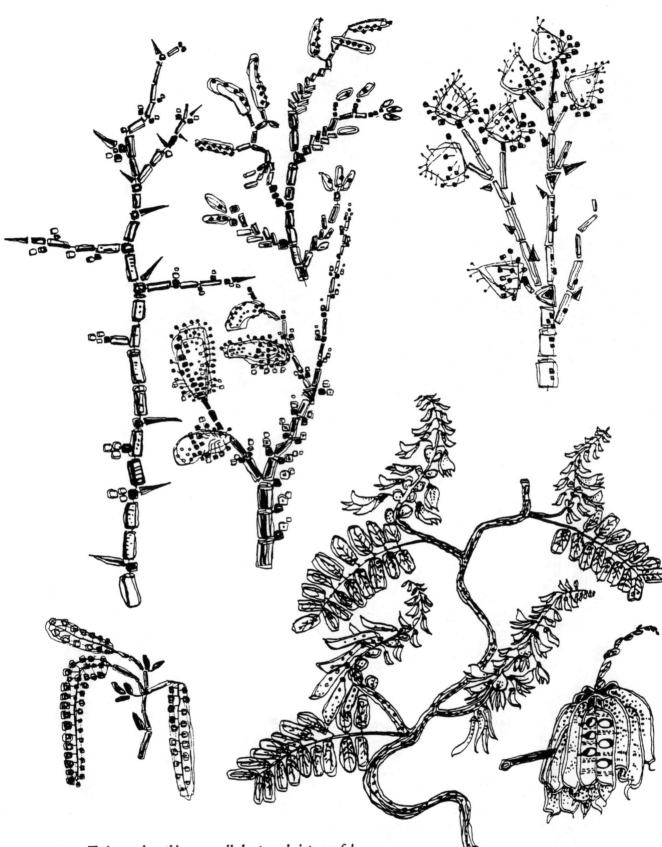

Twigs and catkins can all be turned into useful patterns. If the shadows they cast on a sheet of paper are drawn as a series of dots and dashes, a design in beads and bugles is formed almost automatically

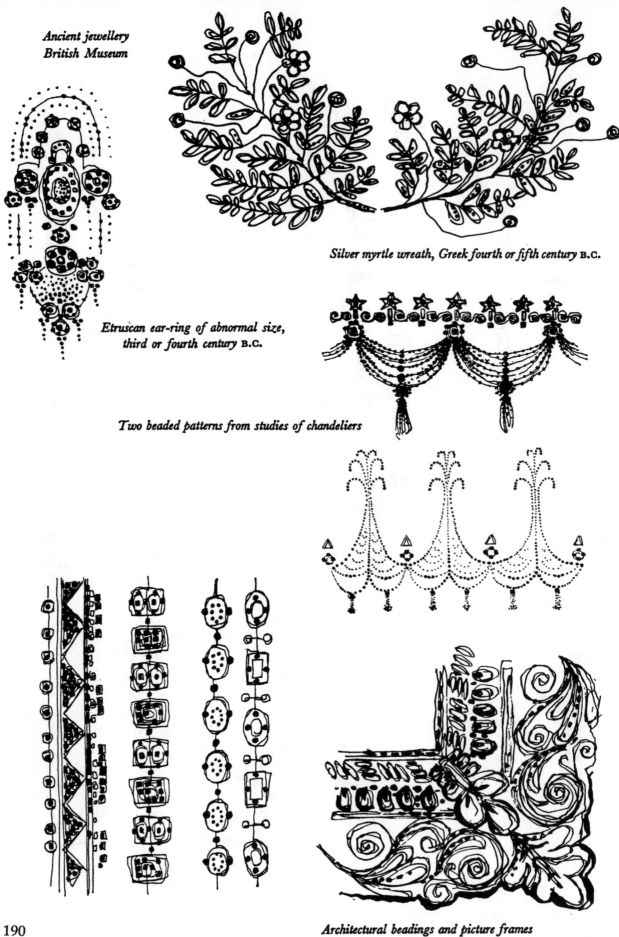

Ancient jewellery British Museum

Silver myrtle wreath, Greek fourth or fifth century B.C.

Etruscan ear-ring of abnormal size, third or fourth century B.C.

Two beaded patterns from studies of chandeliers

190

Architectural beadings and picture frames

About the author

Joan Edwards was born and received her first art school training in Auckland, New Zealand. Having come to England for two years study, she has remained ever since.

She has taught and lectured widely in Britain, The U.S. and New Zealand; is a Fellow of *The Royal Society of Arts*, a member of the *Society of Authors*, the *Society of Designers/Craftsmen*, and the *Embroiderers' Guild*. For ten years she was the Panel Lecturer in Embroidery for the Education Department, Victoria and Albert Museum.

Her writings include articles in *Costume, Embroidery, Garden History*, etc., and several books and papers on embroidery and related topics including, in 1976, a history of Crewel Embroidery. She is currently working on a history of embroidered vestments and furnishings in Britain AD 900 - 1990.

Between 1980 and 1990 Joan and her cousin, Joy Lee, were co-partners in the publication of a series of paperback text books entitled *Joan Edwards' Small Books on the History of Embroidery* which they issued under the imprint Bayford Books. Subsequently they extended the range to include a portfolio of patterns by Joan Drew, *A Picture Book for Kneelermakers* and two biographies, *Dorothy Benson, Machine Embroiderer* and *Textile Graphics of Lilian Dring. Bayford Books* has become a milestone in the literature of embroidery, a successful and rewarding experiment in self-publishing, and an encouraging example for other embroiderers, beaders, and craft-workers to follow.

The barbaric splendour of this figure of the Assyrian goddess Istar who is returning from the underworld carrying her necklace, could be expressed in gold threads, sequins and jewels of all kinds
Drawn from a wall carving, Nimrod Gallery, British Museum

LACIS publishes and distributes books specifically related to the textile arts, focusing on the subjeccts of lace and lace making, costume, embroidery and hand sewing.

Other LACIS books of interest:

EMBROIDERY WITH BEADS, Angela Thompson

BEAD WORK, ed by Jules & Kaethe Kliot

THE ART OF TATTING, Katherine Hoare

TATTING: DESIGNS FROM VICTORIAN LACE CRAFT, Jules & Kaethe Kliot

TATTING WITH VISUAL PATTERNS, Mary Konior

THE ART OF HAIR WORK: HAIR BRAIDING AND THE JEWELRY OF SENTIMENT, Mark Campbell

THE ART OF SHETLAND LACE, Sarah Don

SINGER INSTRUCTIONS FOR ART EMBROIDERY AND LACE WORK, Singer Sewing Machine Co.

GARMENT PATTERNS FOR THE EDWARDIAN LADY, Mrs F. E. Thompson

"STANDARD" WORK ON CUTTING (MEN'S GARMENTS): 1886, Jno. J. Mitchell Co.

THE CARE AND PRESERVATION OF TEXTILES, Karen Finch & Greta Putnam

THE ART OF NETTING, Jules & Kaethe Kliot

MILLINERY FOR EVERY WOMAN, Georgina Kerr Kaye

For a complete list of LACIS titles, write to:

LACIS
3163 Adeline Street
Berkeley, CA 94703
USA